PRAISE FOR

Kitchen Table Wisdom

Winner of the 1996 Wilbur Award
for Best Work of Spiritual Nonfiction

Winner of the Friends of Libraries
USA Readers' Choice Award for 2000

"Dr. Rachel Naomi Remen is a pioneer in the medicine of the future. With the elegance of simplicity, she shows how physicians can become healers by no longer remaining mere technicians of the human body, but by becoming alchemists of the soul."

—Deepak Chopra, M.D.

"Awed by the vitality of the life force . . . Remen tells of those who, having fallen ill, discovered previously untapped wells of fortitude and who, ironically, gained a peace of mind they had never known when well. A heartfelt call for change as well as a display of compassionate and courageous thinking, this meditation will speak especially to those whose lives have been touched by illness."

—*Publishers Weekly*

"Read these gorgeous, from-the-soul stories at the risk of burying cynicism, finding hope, learning a good deal more about life and living—and having a damned good time." —Norman Lear

"Rachel Remen is one of the most important women of our time. She's an extraordinary combination of wounded patient and highly skilled physician, an intuitively compassionate healer, who is also a gifted author and dynamic speaker. She has had a life-changing impact on me." —Naomi Judd

continued . . .

"I love *Kitchen Table Wisdom.* It is a beautiful book. When you read this collection of stories, you will find yourself pausing to remember holy pieces of yourself, when you were awed by the Great Mystery, and glimpsed humanity's relationship to divinity, or felt a deep soul connection with another."

—Jean Shinoda Bolen, M.D.,
author of *Crossing to Avalon*

"[Remen] writes inspirationally about a new vision of healing and living that incorporates the value of the soul. More than a manual on holistic medicine, this collection of case studies takes readers from the beginning of the "life force" through the judgment traps of modern life into an openhearted mystery of embracing life at a friend's table. Refreshingly, her instruction is based on a broader view of medicine that replaces disconnection with celebration of the joy of being a fully healed human" —*Library Journal*

"By telling these stories and encouraging readers to share their own, Remen wants people to see the interconnectedness of human beings and the resilience of the human condition. She does a wonderful job of it." —*Booklist*

KITCHEN TABLE WISDOM

KITCHEN TABLE WISDOM

Stories
That Heal

Rachel Naomi Remen, M.D.

Foreword by Dean Ornish, M.D.

RIVERHEAD BOOKS
NEW YORK

THE BERKLEY PUBLISHING GROUP
Published by the Penguin Group
Penguin Group (USA) Inc.
375 Hudson Street, New York, New York 10014, USA
Penguin Group (Canada), 90 Eglinton Avenue East, Suite 700, Toronto, Ontario M4P 2Y3, Canada (a division of Pearson Penguin Canada Inc.)
Penguin Books Ltd., 80 Strand, London WC2R 0RL, England
Penguin Group Ireland, 25 St. Stephen's Green, Dublin 2, Ireland (a division of Penguin Books Ltd.)
Penguin Group (Australia), 250 Camberwell Road, Camberwell, Victoria 3124, Australia (a division of Pearson Australia Group Pty. Ltd.)
Penguin Books India Pvt. Ltd., 11 Community Centre, Panchsheel Park, New Delhi—110 017, India
Penguin Group (NZ), cnr Airborne and Rosedale Roads, Albany, Auckland 1310, New Zealand (a division of Pearson New Zealand Ltd.)
Penguin Books (South Africa) (Pty.) Ltd., 24 Sturdee Avenue, Rosebank, Johannesburg 2196, South Africa

Penguin Books Ltd., Registered Offices: 80 Strand, London WC2R 0RL, England

The names and identifying characteristics of the persons whose stories are told in this book have been changed to preserve their privacy.

Book design by Lee Fukui

First Riverhead hardcover edition: August 1996
First Riverhead trade paperback edition: August 1997
Riverhead 10th Anniversary Edition: August 2006
Riverhead 10th Anniversary Edition ISBN: 978-1-59448-209-0

The Library of Congress has catalogued the Riverhead hardcover edition as follows:

Remen, Rachel Naomi.
Kitchen table wisdom: stories that heal/Rachel Naomi Remen.
p. cm.
ISBN: 1-57322-042-6
1. Remen, Rachel Naomi. 2. Physicians—United States—Biography. 3. Remen, Rachel Naomi—Philosophy. 4. Meditations. I. Title.
[C]54.R374A3 / 1996
610'.92—dc20 96-5175 CIP
[B]

Printed in the United States of America

10 9 8

CONTENTS

For everyone who has never told their story

PREFACE TO THE 10TH ANNIVERSARY EDITION

Like everything else, this book has a story.

Kitchen Table Wisdom was sold on the basis of a single little story that a friend of mine encouraged me to send to his book agent, who in turn sold it to a publisher. There was no book proposal, no book theme, no chapter outline. Not the way in which a publisher is accustomed to buy a book. An editor was assigned to take me in hand and put things right.

"Let us make an outline," she said firmly.

Unfortunately, I am not a person capable of making outlines. After an hour or so of working together, she admitted defeat.

"What is this book about?" she asked.

I did not know.

"Rachel," she said. "When you meet a new counseling patient, surely you identify their problem, decide what to do and in what order you need to do it, and make a plan, don't you?"

I had felt exposed.

"No," I said. "I don't know what people need to do or who they need to become. When I first meet with someone, I have no idea where we are going, and where we end up is usually a surprise to us both."

She sat back in dismay. "Then how do you get quality outcomes?" she asked.

"I just follow the natural process of things," I mumbled, avoiding her eye.

My editor is one of the best in the business, and she rose to the occasion. She smiled her encouragement and said the thing that made *Kitchen Table Wisdom* possible. "Just write about whatever matters to you, Rachel. Give me four hundred pages by this time next year and we will figure out together what the book is about."

And that was the beginning.

I quickly discovered that I am an author and not a writer. Writers are people who are probably born to write. An author, on the other hand, seems to be born to do something else and then writes a book about it. This is a very different thing entirely. Caught up in the routine of daily life as a physician, I had not planned to write a book. But my story had attracted the attention of my friend's agent and she sent it to a publisher who was willing to take a chance. The publisher offered me a contract and suddenly I was an author. I did not feel ready.

In a panic I called a friend who has written several books, and she recommended a woman who she had hired to help her write. My meeting with this woman did not go well. Lunch was pleasant enough, but after the tea was poured she looked me in the eye.

"Do you want someone to write this book for you?" she asked.

"No," I said. "I'd like to give it a try myself."

She paused. I could tell that this was not the answer she had hoped for.

"Well," she said, "remember that you are not a writer. So only write about the things you know." Patting her lips with her napkin, she rose from the table, shook my hand, and left.

I had felt diminished by her words and dismissed by her tone. Now, ten years afterward, I am deeply grateful for her advice.

Because I am not a writer, when I sat down to write, all I had were my memories. The stories I had lived through and the stories I had shared. The stories people had told me in the supermarket, on airplanes and in the ladies room. So I told my computer a story. And then another. And another. When the manuscript deadline arrived, I had four hundred pages of little stories.

I was mortified that this was all that I had to show after a year of work. In the world of medicine, where things that can be expressed in numbers are considered truer than things that can only be expressed in words, stories are considered poor form and storytellers are highly suspect. My tendency to tell stories had always been frowned upon by my medical colleagues and rejected as "anecdotal evidence." They preferred to measure truth in terms of hard data. So I had learned to keep my stories to myself.

Embarrassed, I called my editor to say that I had missed the deadline but I was sending over what I had. I apologized and added that I thought I now knew what the book was about: It was a book about healing, and I had written all the case histories for it. I expected that it would take me another six weeks to actually write the book itself, but I was starting now. She called me back in two days.

"Stop writing," she said.

"Why?" I asked, surprised.

"Because it's finished," she told me.

"It's a book of little stories?" I asked, appalled.

"Yes," she said, "and a book about stories."

I was speechless. "But I can't publish a book of stories."

"Why not?" she asked, mystified.

"Because it has no footnotes," I stammered in great distress.

"Why does it need footnotes?" she asked me.

I was almost in tears. "If it has no footnotes it will have no credibility."

She paused. "Rachel," she said very gently, "I think that you are going to discover something important about credibility." And I have.

I did write only about the things I know; what I have learned from being the child of my parents and my grandparents and from the thousands of people I have cared for in the forty-four years I have been a doctor. What I have learned from living with an incurable illness called Crohn's disease for more than fifty-three years. What I have thought about in the middle of the night. I wrote about these sorts of things because they were all that I had. I discovered that they are all that anyone has, and they are enough. In the end, I write about something I know intimately: that every one of us matters. And that we have the power to befriend and strengthen the life in one another and to change the world, one heart at a time.

Authors do not expect to be authors. We do not take it easily in stride. For the whole twelve months that I was writing down the stories in *Kitchen Table Wisdom,* I was in a state of disbelief and doubt. When the pre-publication copy of the book arrived in the mail, I carried it with me everywhere. I even slept with it under my pillow. The idea that there would soon be thousands of copies of it troubled me. The very personal nature of the book made me feel vulnerable and exposed. Had I been able to pay back the publisher's advance, I would have bought back the manuscript, but I had spent the money and I had to go forward. As the publication date approached I couldn't sleep or eat. But the date passed. Slowly I began to relax. No one had noticed.

A few weeks after the book was published, I was in a bookstore looking for something to read. Seeing a clerk helping a middle-aged woman among the shelves, I stood behind her and waited my turn to ask for help. He climbed a short ladder and handed her down a book. She thanked him and hesitated.

"Do you have a copy of *Kitchen Table Wisdom*?" she asked.

Standing a few feet behind her, I did something a seasoned writer would never do. I gasped.

Turning, she smiled at me. "Oh, have you read it?" she asked me.

Somehow I managed to blurt out that I had written it. There was a moment of silence and then she reached out to me and touched my arm.

"I was diagnosed with cancer a few months ago," she told me. "Your book has helped me and I am buying it for someone who also has cancer."

I had tears in my eyes. "How did it help you?" I asked.

She smiled again. "I am less afraid," she said.

Now, ten years later, I too am less afraid, less apologetic. When I wrote *Kitchen Table Wisdom,* I had no idea what it would come to mean to people, about the way it would reach people and strengthen them, the way it would touch people and make them feel less alone. I have discovered the power of story to change people. I have seen a story heal shame and free people from fear, ease suffering and restore a lost sense of worth. I have learned that the ways we can befriend and strengthen the life in one another are very simple and very old. Stories have not lost their power to heal over generations. Stories need no footnotes.

Since *Kitchen Table Wisdom* was published, I have learned that the things that divide us are far less important than those that connect us. I have traveled throughout the country and read stories to people in hundreds of bookstores. I have received letters from grandmothers and schoolchildren, from CEOs and construction workers, from nurses and doctors and people who are sick. I have read every one of the many thousands of letters that I have received. I have heard people's dreams and fears and seen their courage. I have become prouder to be a human being.

I have glimpsed the true size of the kitchen table at which we sit and that we all have our places at it. I am grateful to know that I, too, have a place.

There has been a great deal of grace in the writing of this book. I am thankful that my stories have helped others find a deeper satisfaction in their lives and discover they are more without becoming different. I, too, am more without becoming different.

I feel blessed.

Rachel Naomi Remen, M.D.
Mill Valley, California, 2006

FOREWORD

Whenever I give a lecture at a scientific meeting, speakers are asked to sign a form revealing whether or not there is a potential conflict of interest. So, in the spirit of full disclosure, let me say right up front that Dr. Rachel Naomi Remen is one of my dearest friends and one of the most extraordinary people I know.

I love Rachel. And by the time you finish reading this book, there's a good chance that you will, too.

Great artists in any field have the rare ability to see our world and our lives anew, to experience life directly without it being filtered through beliefs, expectations, and preconceptions. They can recapture a lost sense of wonder and experience the full richness of life. Even more uncommon is the ability to put that vision and experience into words so that we, too, can learn to see with new eyes and feel again with an open heart.

The ability to experience the familiar in new ways does not require extreme life-and-death situations; it can occur even in daily life. Perhaps *especially* in ordinary experiences. For example, I recently ordered some pasta and vegetables with tomato sauce. The sauce tasted different, not at all like what I was expecting. It had a wonderful flavor; familiar, but I couldn't place it. Because I couldn't name it, I couldn't limit it. I had no category in which to put it, so I was able to experience it directly. My mouth almost exploded in rich flavor. I finally realized it was just hickory sauce. It was the same hickory sauce I'd had many times before, but it was an entirely different experience.

Names and beliefs and preconceptions can bring a sense of order to the world, but often at the expense of being able to experience life fully. Rachel Remen's rare gift is to help us see beyond the veil of our beliefs and our judgments of ourselves and others and see the world with wonder and wisdom, as if for the first time.

She sees from the perspective of a patient with a forty-year history of a chronic illness. She sees from the vantage point of an extremely well trained and accomplished physician. And she sees from the point of view of a counselor.

She is all of these, and more. Rachel Remen is someone who fits in everywhere and yet nowhere, like an anthropologist in her own culture and a visionary in her own profession. She is a warrior of compassion and a sorceress of the spirit.

Spiritual teachers come in many guises. Sometimes they come in the guise of physicians like Rachel, sometimes in the guise of ordinary people who are suffering with disease. To learn to hear the spiritual teaching that all of us can offer to each other is what this book is about.

The wisdom in this book is grounded in real life. Rachel does not write, "this is the way." Her wisdom emerges more organically. She can hear and transmit the message of the ultimate spiritual teacher, which is life itself.

Life is full of the unknown, full of wonder, full of mystery. Most books try to lead you out of mystery into mastery. Rachel Remen's book leads us to recognize and move toward the mystery that is in everyday life. Moving into the unknown is often where we find the healing, not by running away from it into a quick fix. She teaches that life is not broken and does not need to be fixed; it needs to be savored and celebrated.

As a scientist, I live in a world of data, numbers, randomized controlled clinical trials. Scientists believe what can be measured—blood pressure, cholesterol, blood flow—even though, as Dr. Denis Burkit once said, "Not everything that counts can be counted." Anecdotal evidence—in other words, stories—is viewed with suspicion by scientists. There are too many confounding variables, so the facts are harder to prove, to replicate.

But there is no meaning in facts. As a physician, and as a human being, I live in a world of stories. Stories are not replicable because our lives are unique. Our uniqueness is what gives us value and meaning. Yet in the telling of stories we also learn what makes us similar, what connects us all, what helps us transcend the isolation that separates us from each other and from ourselves.

Stories are the language of community. The heart is a pump

and needs to be treated on a physical level with the best medicine that science has to offer, but we are more than just machines. The real epidemic in our culture is not just physical heart disease; it's what I call emotional and spiritual heart disease: the sense of loneliness, isolation, and alienation that is so prevalent in our culture because of the breakdown of the social networks that used to give us a sense of connection and community.

So what? People who feel lonely and isolated are more likely to smoke, to overeat, to abuse drugs, to work too hard. Also, many studies have shown that people who feel lonely and isolated have three to five times the risk of premature death not only from heart disease but also from *all* causes when compared to those who have a sense of connection and community.

In my work, I often find that there is a great hunger for a sense of connection and community. Many people who enter our programs often come to lower their cholesterol levels, reduce blood pressure, lose weight, or, as they often put it, to "unclog their arteries." They come expecting to change their diet, to stop smoking, to exercise.

I have learned that providing people with health information—facts—is important but not usually sufficient to motivate them to make lasting changes in diet and lifestyle. If it were, no one would smoke. We need to work at a deeper level.

Part of our program is what we call "group support," which began as a place that felt safe enough for people to exchange recipes and shopping tips but which evolved into a community, a place that felt safe enough for people to talk about what was really going on in their lives—to tell their stories—without fear of being judged, abandoned, or criticized. Although this is the part of our program that many people have difficulty with, they usually find it to be the most meaningful. When we work at that level, we often find that people are much more likely to make lifestyle changes that are life-enhancing rather than ones that are self-destructive.

Suffering—whether physical, emotional, spiritual, or as often the case, all three—can be a doorway to transformation. As we move to the end of this century and millennium, our personal suffering is sometimes worsened by the lack of communication and community. Illness often intensifies these feelings of isolation.

Telling stories can be healing. We all have within us access to a greater wisdom, and we may not even know that until we speak out loud.

Listening to stories also can be healing. A deep trust of life often emerges when you listen to other people's stories. You realize you're not alone; you're traveling in wonderful company. Ordinary people living ordinary lives often are heroes.

Reading Rachel Remen's book can be healing. In hearing her voice and the voices of those who have used their wounds as doorways for transforming their pain, somehow along the way our suffering subsides, our wounds begin healing, our hearts begin to feel safe enough to open a little wider.

The connection to each other and to our soul and spirit is already there. During the times that we feel most vulnerable, that which is invulnerable within us becomes uncovered, becomes more apparent. When our hearts begin to open, we are able to feel it, like opening the window shade and letting in the sunshine that's been there all along, waiting patiently to be allowed inside.

Dean Ornish, M.D.
President and Director
Preventive Medicine Research Institute
Sausalito, California
March 4, 1996

INTRODUCTION

My grandfather had early on, in a manner worthy of Socrates himself, engaged me in the search for what is Real. His world, inhabited by an immanent and personal god, was one of the two worlds of my childhood. He was a grave and scholarly man, elderly by the time that I was born, an orthodox rabbi who spent much of his time studying the texts of mystical Judaism. The books of the Kabala he had brought with him from Russia were old, written out by hand in Hebrew on very thin paper. As a small child, I would sit under the table as he studied them, stroking his purple velvet carpet slippers and daydreaming.

The other world of my childhood was the world of medicine. Among two generations of my grandfather's children there are three nurses and nine physicians. When I was young I thought you became an adult and a doctor as part of the same process. I learned early the right thing to say when I was asked what I wanted to be when I grew up. I was the only pre-med in kindergarten. When my grandfather died he left me in his will the money to go to medical school. I was seven years old.

As I grew older, the weight of these family expectations began to grow heavy. My uncles and cousins were men of science, distant, cultured, intellectual, and successful. Like my father, they rewarded me for having the right answers. My grandfather had rewarded me for having the right questions. I admired these doctors but I had loved my grandfather and his way of questioning life. At twelve, my closest male cousin and I both wanted to be rabbis. We both became doctors.

I think I ultimately chose medicine because of a novel I read when I was about twelve, a story about the life of Saint Luke called *The Road to Bithynia*. Historical novels were the LSD of the fifties, an easy escape for a generation of bored postwar adolescents. I was addicted to them.

I had not known that Luke was a physician. *The Road to Bithynia* had originally appealed to me because the Gospel According to Luke was my favorite part of the Christmas story. The book was written by a physician, Frank Slaughter, who told Luke's story with all the power and credibility of his own personal knowledge of the practice of medicine. I read the novel four times, stunned to find that all physicians were not like my uncles, that it might be possible to be a physician in a way that my grandfather would have understood. That being a physician could become a means to better know and serve life and the source of life. The novel offered the hope that someone like myself might find a place in medicine, without needing to choose between my grandfather's way of life and that of his sons.

The day it all began stands out in my memory: my father

carrying my belongings to my room at the medical student residence, my mother unpacking my clothes and lining my drawers with special paper as always, working as partners until there was nothing left to do. I remember the uneasy conversation and at last closing the door behind them. How much they had wanted to stay, to share in this last-night-before-the-first-day of medical school. But at twenty, I had wanted to face this momentous thing by myself.

I looked at the carefully folded clothes, the shelves empty of books, the hard and narrow bed, and the bare surface of the desk. The room felt impersonal, monastic even, very different from the feminine bedroom I had slept in the night before. It would be my home for four years. Tonight it felt cold and somehow unsafe.

I felt a familiar doubt, a fear that I was doing the wrong thing, that I was not cut out for this and would fail at it. As a philosophy major, I had barely been admitted to Cornell's school of medicine. The interviewer had looked at my honors degree in Wittgensteinian philosophy, commented that my major was "irrelevant," and entered into a brisk discussion of genetics, his own life work. I had held my own, but secretly I knew I was no scientist. Secretly, I found science colorless and cold. Full of hard edges. Like this room.

Hugging myself, I turned toward the only window. Earlier, I had glanced out and noticed that it looked onto the city street. I had a brief impression of unrelieved grayness. But it was night now and there across the street was the main entrance of the hospital, one of the best-known in the world. It was blazing with light.

From where I stood I could see the main building and the

two wings enclosing the great semicircular driveway. An endless flow of cars came and went, bringing sick people, people in trouble, and those to whom they mattered. I stepped to the window deciding to watch for a while, just until the lights went out. A little before midnight a crowd of people, many wearing white, arrived and a little after midnight a great many other white-clad people left and found their way to their cars in the parking lots. The shift had changed. I got the blanket from the bed, wrapped myself in it, and pulled up a chair. Cars, ambulances, taxis, and police cars continued to come and go. I nodded off several times, awakening each time to find nothing had changed. By four A.M. I realized that these lights never went out. People were there, always, for anyone in crisis, anyone in pain. The lights were being passed from hand to hand. And as of this morning, I was a part of this. I knew nothing yet, but I belonged.

In my grandfather's synagogue there was a light that never went out. All synagogues have such an eternal light. It signifies that the unseen presence of God is always in this place. Comforted, I got up and went to sleep. Over the next four years I can't remember ever having the time to look out that window again.

It is not possible to be in a twenty-four-hour-a-day intensive training program for many years and not be changed by it. We worked seven days a week, thirty-six straight hours on and twelve hours off, for most of it. When we were off we slept. Denial of the body, its needs for sleep, comfort, and even food, was the very foundation of the schedule. No one complained. It was just the way that we all lived. Many of the rooms I worked and studied in had no windows. Often I did not know what day it was or even the time. I remember watching the nursing shift going past me, day after day. I would look up and see Miss Harrison and know it must be morning again. Often I had not slept since I had last seen her. Once during my internship, my mother, visiting me in the house staff residence, was horrified to open my closet and find that I did not have a winter coat. "Where is your coat?" she gasped. I had not known it was winter. I had not been outside the hospital and its underground tunnel systems in over a year.

On one very rare summer afternoon off I remember traveling home to visit my parents on the subway, realizing only after a while that I had been unconsciously scanning the veins of the bare-armed people around me, wondering whether my skills with a needle were good enough to allow me to successfully draw blood from them. This sort of training changes the way you see things, the way you think. Gradually things that had been central in my previous life became vague and faded into the background and other things more heavily rewarded became overdeveloped. After a time I just forgot many important things.

Thirty-five years ago, I was one of a few women in my training program and my male colleagues generally assumed that, as a woman, I had a greater comfort and skill in meeting the emotional needs of patients. Actually, at the time nothing could have been farther from the truth. In many ways I was emotionally less well developed than some of the men I worked with daily. Throughout four years of medical school I had competed successfully with men and had fiercely and single-mindedly cultivated the very qualities of decisiveness, objectivity, competence, judgment, and analytical thinking that were most respected in this culture. These qualities had become even more important to me than to the men as I struggled to overcome what was widely perceived by them to be a gender handicap.

Yet sometimes the same teammates who so painstakingly treated me as if I were a man called on me in situations that made them uncomfortable. When we were all working the clinic or the emergency room, each seeing patients in our own examining rooms, there would be a knock on my door. Opening it, I would find another doctor standing there ill at ease, who would say something like, "My patient is crying . . . can you come?" I was no more comfortable than he in such situations but I realized early that this was part of my ticket to acceptance and so I would go and listen while someone shared with me their concerns and their experience of actually living with the disease we had diagnosed.

At first, I was surprised that people with the same disease had such very different stories. Later I became deeply moved by these stories, by the people and the meaning they found in their problems, by the unsuspected strengths, the depths of love and devotion, the rich and human tapestry initiated by the pathology I was studying and treating. Eventually, these stories would become far more compelling to me than the disease process. I would come to feel more personally enriched by them than by making the correct diagnosis. They would make me proud to be a human being.

These stories engaged me at another, more hidden point. I too suffer from an illness, Crohn's disease, a chronic, progressive intestinal disease which I had developed at the age of fifteen.

So for me, these conversations eased a certain loneliness. This was a different sort of connection than the easy banter and camaraderie I enjoyed with the other medical residents. This was the conversation of people in bomb shelters, people under siege, people in times of common crisis everywhere. I listened to human beings who were suffering, and responding to their suffering in ways as unique as their fingerprints. Their stories were inspiring, moving, important. In time, the truth in them began to heal me.

Everybody is a story. When I was a child, people sat around kitchen tables and told their stories. We don't do that so much anymore. Sitting around the table telling stories is not just a way of passing time. It is the way the wisdom gets passed along. The stuff that helps us to live a life worth remembering. Despite the awesome powers of technology many of us still do not live very well. We may need to listen to each other's stories once again.

Most of the stories we are told now are written by novelists and screenwriters, acted out by actors and actresses, stories that have beginnings and endings, stories that are not real. The stories we can tell each other have no beginning and ending. They are a front-row seat to the real experience. Even though they may have happened in a different time or place they have a familiar feel. In some way they are about us, too.

Real stories take time. We stopped telling stories when we started to lose that sort of time, pausing time, reflecting time, wondering time. Life rushes us along and few people are strong enough to stop on their own. Most often, something unforeseen stops us and it is only then we have the time to take a seat at life's kitchen table. To know our own story and tell it. To listen to other people's stories. To remember that the real world is made of just such stories.

Until we stop ourselves or, more often, have been stopped, we hope to put certain of life's events "behind us" and get on with our living. After we stop we see that certain of life's issues will be with us for as long as we live. We will pass through them again and again, each time with a new story, each time with a greater understanding, until they become indistinguishable from our blessings and our wisdom. It's the way life teaches us how to live.

When we haven't the time to listen to each other's stories we seek out experts to tell us how to live. The less time we spend together at the kitchen table, the more how-to books appear in the stores and on our bookshelves. But reading such books is a very different thing than listening to someone's lived experience. Because we have stopped listening to each other we may even have forgotten how to listen, stopped learning how to recognize meaning and fill ourselves from the ordinary events of our lives. We have become solitary; readers and watchers rather than sharers and participants.

The kitchen table is a level playing field. Everyone's story matters. The wisdom in the story of the most educated and powerful person is often not greater than the wisdom in the story of a child, and the life of a child can teach us as much as the life of a sage.

Most parents know the importance of telling children their own story, over and over again, so that they come to know in the tellings who they are and to whom they belong. At the kitchen table we do this for each other. Hidden in all stories is the One story. The more we listen, the clearer that Story becomes. Our true identity, who we are, why we are here, what sustains us, is in this story. The stories at every kitchen table are about the same things, stories of owning, having and losing, stories of sex, of power, of pain, of wounding, of courage, hope, and healing, of loneliness and the end of loneliness. Stories about God.

In telling them, we are telling each other the human story. Stories that touch us in this place of common humanness awaken us and weave us together as a family once again.

Sometimes when I ask people to tell me their story they tell me about their achievements, what they have acquired or built over a lifetime. So many of us do not know our own story. A story about who we are, not what we have done. About what we have faced to build what we have built, what we have drawn upon and risked to do it, what we have felt, thought, feared, and discovered through the events of our lives. The real story that belongs to us alone.

All real stories are true. Sometimes when a patient tells me their story, someone in their family will protest. "But it didn't happen quite that way, it happened more like this." Over the years I have come to know that the stories both these people tell me are equally true, equally genuine, and that neither of them may be "correct," an exact description of the event much as a video camera might have recorded it. Stories are someone's experience of the events of their life, they are not the events themselves. Most of us experience the same event very differently. We have seen it in our own unique way and the story we tell has more than a bit of ourselves in it. Truth is highly subjective.

All stories are full of bias and uniqueness; they mix fact with meaning. This is the root of their power. Stories allow us to see something familiar through new eyes. We become in that moment a guest in someone else's life, and together with them sit at the feet of their teacher. The meaning we may draw from someone's story may be different from the meaning they themselves have drawn. No matter. Facts bring us to knowledge, but stories lead to wisdom.

The best stories have many meanings; their meaning changes as our capacity to understand and appreciate meaning grows. Revisiting such stories over the years, one wonders how one could not have seen their present meaning all along, all the time unaware of what meaning a future reading may hold. Like the stories themselves, all these meanings are true.

Knowing your own story requires having a personal response to life, an inner experience of life. It is possible to live a life without experiencing it. Most children experience life more fully than we do. Children are aware of the particulars. For a child the time between Halloween and Christmas is made up of thousands and thousands of fully experienced moments. That takes longer to live through, longer to go by. After forty, Christmas seems to come three times a year.

I was once a pediatrician but I am no longer; for many years now I have listened to the stories of people with cancer and other life-threatening illnesses as their counselor. From them I have learned how to enjoy the minute particulars in life once again, the grace of a hot cup of coffee, the presence of a friend, the blessing of having a new cake of soap or an hour without pain. Such humble experience is the stuff that many of the very best stories are made of. If we think we have no stories it is because we have not paid enough attention to our lives. Most of us live lives that are far richer and more meaningful than we appreciate.

We carry with us every story we have ever heard and every story we have ever lived, filed away at some deep place in our memory. We carry most of those stories unread, as it were, until we have grown the capacity or the readiness to read them. When that happens they may come back to us filled with a previously unsuspected meaning. It is almost as if we have been collecting pieces of a greater wisdom, sometimes over many years without knowing.

My mother was a woman who was full of stories. As a public-health visiting nurse, she had sat at many kitchen tables, drinking tea and listening. At the age of eighty-four she chose to have cardiac bypass surgery, because it was the last chance she had for life. Even so, the odds were long: four chances in ten that she would not survive the operation. But my mother was not your ordinary elderly lady. She had lived her life as a maverick and a risk taker and to her those odds looked good. The morning of her surgery, I came to her hospital room two hours early only to find that her surgery had been moved forward and I was barely in time to kiss her before they took her upstairs. Despite the sudden change in plans and the daunting odds she was facing, my mother was peaceful, even radiant.

"Oh good!" she greeted me. "You're here! There was something that I wanted to tell you. I wanted to be certain you knew that no matter what happens here, *I am satisfied* and I hope you will do whatever you can to be satisfied as well." Then she smiled her charming, rakish smile and they took her away. These were her final lucid words to me.

For a long time I thought about these words, trying to understand what they had meant. My mother had achieved a great deal in her life but I did not think it was this that had given her such ease and contentment in the face of possible death. Slowly I have come to understand that the key to this sort of satisfaction lies in the inner world, the world of stories and memories. It comes not from any outer achievement but from the richness of experiencing life and sharing the inner experience of life with others.

After thirty-five years of being a physician and more than forty years of living with my own life-threatening illness, I too am a woman who is full of stories. Stories I have lived and stories I have been told. I have stories about being a daughter, a granddaughter, a friend. Stories about being a patient and stories about being a doctor. Stories other doctors and patients have told me. Stories about my cat. Stories about things I do not understand. If I were sitting at your kitchen table the way a family physician used to do, these are some of the stories I would bring there with me.

Every one of these stories has helped me to live.

KITCHEN TABLE WISDOM

I.

Life Force

COHERENT, ELEGANT, mysterious, aesthetic. When I first earned my degree in medicine I would not have described life in this way. But I was not on intimate terms with life then. I had not seen the power of the life force in everyone, met the will to live in all its varied and subtle forms, recognized the irrepressible love of life buried in the heart of every living thing. I had not been used by life to fulfill itself or been caught unaware by its strength in the midst of the most profound weakness. I had no sense of awe. I had thought that life was broken and that I, armed with the powerful tools of modern science, would fix it. I had thought then that I was broken also. But life has shown me otherwise.

Many of the people who come to my office now as counseling clients have come because modern medicine has failed them in some way, or they have used up its power to help them and they do not know what else to do. They hope to find a way to heal, to cooperate with or even strengthen the life in them. After listening to hundreds and hundreds of their stories over the last twenty years I think I would have to say that most people do not recognize the strength of the life force in them or the many ways that it shows itself to them. Yet every one of us has felt its power. We who doubt are covered with the scars of our many healings.

So when people first come, this is the place we usually start—talking about life itself, our attitude toward it, our experience of it, our trust or distrust of it. Developing an eye to see it, in others and in ourselves. In the beginning is the life force. After more than fifty years of living, I have learned it can be trusted.

PLUM BLOSSOMS

MANY YEARS AGO in the midst of a shopping trip, I found myself in a store specializing in Japanese furniture, helping a friend who was furnishing his house. He had been rapidly taken over by the only salesperson, a tiny woman in a kimono who had grabbed his arm and begun a discussion of Japanese paintings with him in a loud and intense voice. Her head reached barely above his elbow but in spite of her size her manner made me uncomfortable and I drifted away toward the door, lurking behind chests and tonkus, waiting until he finished his purchases. I thought I had hidden successfully until, without warning, the woman turned and moved toward me, pointing as she came. I saw then that she was very old, possibly even deaf, and this perhaps explained her loudness. She took me by the arm and began to pull me through the showroom, encouraging me with little clicking noises and repetitions of "Come. You come." I tried to shake her off but for someone so small and frail her grip was strong. So I went along, followed by my friend, who was clearly amused by my struggle.

She took us into a room in the back of the store, empty except for four scrolls, one on each wall, representing the seasons. Unlike the paintings in the showroom these were museum-quality. In one of them, an old and twisted branch bloomed with hundreds of tiny pink blossoms. The branch and the blossoms were covered with snow. It was exquisite.

Leading me up to this, she said to me, "You see, you see? February! The plum blossom comes!" In her odd intense way she told me that the plum suffered because it was the first, it bloomed early, in February, often still in winter, in the hard and the cold. She touched the snow on the branch with her small arthritic hand, nodding her head vigorously. Looking intensely into my face and shaking my arm slightly, she said, "Plum blossom, the beginning. Like Japanese woman, plum blossom gentle, tender, soft . . . and survive."

I puzzled about this for a long time afterwards. As a physician, I thought I knew about survival, because after all I was in the survival business. I had known survival to be a matter of expertise, of skill and action, of competence and knowledge. What she had told me made no sense to me.

This was confusing to me for other reasons as well. Like the plum blossoms, I too had come early. My mother had suffered from toxemia and I had been delivered by emergency cesarean section far below full-term weight. In February 1938, I had not been expected to live. All through my childhood I had been told that I had survived because of the invention of the incubator. For many years I had felt grateful for this technology, dependent upon it for my life. Now as a young pediatrician I was working in a premature intensive-care nursery using far more powerful technology to keep other babies alive. But what the old woman had said had made me wonder. Perhaps survival was not only a question of the skillful use of state-of-the-art technology, perhaps there was something innate, some strength in those tiny pink infants, that enabled both them and me to survive. I had never thought of that before.

It reminded me of something that had happened one spring day when I was fourteen. Walking up Fifth Avenue in New York City, I was astonished to notice two tiny blades of grass growing through the sidewalk. Green and tender, they had somehow broken through the cement. Despite the crowds bumping up against me, I stopped and looked at them in disbelief. This image stayed with me for a long time, possibly because it seemed so miraculous to me. At the time, my idea of power was very different. I understood the power of knowledge, of wealth, of government, and the law. I had no experience with this other sort of power yet.

Accidents and natural disasters often cause people to feel that life is fragile. In my experience, life can change abruptly and end without warning, but life is not fragile. There is a difference between impermanence and fragility. Even on the physiological level, the body is an intricate design of checks and balances, elegant strategies of survival layered on strategies of survival, balances and rebalances. Anyone who has witnessed the recovery from such massive and invasive interventions as bone marrow transplant or open heart surgery comes away with a sense of deep respect, if not awe, for the ability of the body to survive. This is as true in age as it is in youth. There is a tenacity toward life which is present at the intracellular level without which even the most sophisticated of medical interventions would not succeed. The drive to live is strong even in the most tiny of human beings. I remember as a medical student seeing one of my teachers put a finger in the mouth of a newborn and, once the baby took hold, gently lift him partway off the bed by the strength of his suck.

That tenacity toward life endures in all of us, undiminished, until the moment of our death.

THE WILL TO LIVE

CAN WE CHOOSE TO LIVE? And if so, do we choose survival in the same way that we choose a suit of clothes or a car? Many people have come to believe that we do. Yet evidence suggests that survival may not be chosen quite in the same way that we choose a possession. Life is not a possession. Those who intensely wish to live sometimes may die and others, for whom life has little appeal, often linger on. How strange when many of us have an inner experience that there is some dimension of personal choice connected to survival.

In these years of observing survival, I have come to wonder if there isn't a will accessed in dreams and imagery that is a part of some basic encoding at the very center of our personal lives. Here at this deep unconscious level lies the drive to remain incarnate for purposes unknown to the conscious mind, a sort of commitment of our personal life force toward the particular and the concrete. Perhaps hidden in the present debate about personal choice and ultimate survival is an older, more mysterious concept which has been called the will to live.

If this is so, many factors on the unconscious level of things may affect this will, its strength, its coherence, and its tenacity. Our deepest and most unconscious beliefs about our own essential nature, our worthiness to live, may be operating here. Sometimes a kink in the will to live becomes most clear only when someone is challenged by significant illness.

Max was the sort of man who lived close to the edge, smoking, drinking, fighting, driving fast cars. He was there wherever the edge was. At sixty-three, he had been married four times and had made and lost two fortunes. At present he was a successful cattle breeder. He sat in my office, in a ten-gallon hat and battered boots, as uncomfortable and uneasy here as one of his own beloved champion bulls, penned up too small. In response to my questions about his past, he told me he had grown up on a ranch in the Midwest. His father had been a cowboy, his mother the only daughter of the town banker. He had been close to his mother. His older brother, a robust and fearless child, had been close to their father. Their father had loved him, he said, and looked away.

I looked at him sitting there, large and competent and reckless-looking. His hands, resting on his denimed knees, were scarred from a lifetime of outdoor work. They were a man's hands. Why then did I have this stab of protectiveness, this fleeting sense of him as a frail little boy? Following this hunch, I asked him what he knew of his own birth and early childhood. He told me he had been born prematurely. For the first two or three years of his life he was sickly and had absorbed a great deal of his mother's attention, worry, and time. His father's frustration had built until in one violent argument with his mother he had told her, "If that little runt was one of the animals, I'd have put it out to starve." I asked if he had overheard this or had been told about it by someone. He could not remember, he said, but he'd always known it and he knew beyond doubt that it had happened.

His father's resentment toward him had remained unchanged even after he had become big and made himself physically tough. "He was not a forgiving man," he said. Sometimes his father would not speak to him or acknowledge his presence for weeks, acting as if he were not there at all. He never knew why. It had been no easy childhood and at fifteen Max had left home.

Annoyed with my questions, he asked me why all this was important. His foot was tapping and his eyes were restless. He patted his pockets absently. I wondered if he was yearning for a smoke. I told him that people's attitudes toward themselves sometimes made it easier or harder to recover their health and so it was good to understand as much as we could.

He began to talk then about his self-destructive tendencies. He told me that he had "pushed death" for as long as he could remember, and described years of hard living and numerous injuries. Even as a child he had been accident-prone and this had diverted even more of his mother's attention toward him and fed his father's resentment. He did not understand why this was so as he was athletic and well coordinated. "I always felt like I was no account, like I was no good." His many successes, in business or in sports or with women, had not eased these feelings but just covered them over. "Fooled 'em all," he said grimly. "Perhaps," I said, "it was hard to feel okay because you could never be sure just what you needed to do to be okay." He looked at me, puzzled. "If you were supposed to live to please your mother, or die to please your dad," I said.

My remark shocked him. He had often wondered if he had lived recklessly in order to win his father's approval or to prove himself the tougher man. This put a new spin on it. "From the moment I was born, I was a real thorn in his side just because I was there. Nothing I could do made a difference. He didn't want me anyhow."

I reminded him that despite his many brushes with death, the broken bones, the accidents, the risks he took almost daily, he was still here. I asked him what he thought had brought him through. "Luck," he said quickly. I shot him a skeptical look. No one was that lucky. He sat for a while with his thoughts. Then in a choked and almost inaudible voice, he told me that he himself had always wanted to live. I could hardly hear him. "Can you say that any louder?" He looked at the rug between his boots. Unable to speak, he just nodded. Almost in a whisper he said, "I feel ashamed."

My heart went out to him. In a shaking voice he said, "Something in me wants to live." His eyes were still fixed on the rug. "Say it, Max," I thought. "Say it until it becomes real." I wondered if I dared to push him a little further. "Do you think you could look at me and tell me that?" I asked him. I could sense the struggle in him. Had I gone too far? He had never confronted his father. Most likely, saying such a simple thing out loud went against a lifelong pattern. Perhaps he would not be able to free himself even this little bit. With an effort he raised his eyes, his voice still choked but no longer inaudible. "I want to live," he said evenly. We stared at each other for a few moments but he did not drop his eyes. I smiled at him. "I want you to live too," I said.

One way of looking at Max's history would be that the old argument between his parents had continued on in his unconscious mind. Confused and caught between his mother's commitment to his life and his father's wish that he disappear, he had ridden the fence between life and death all these years. Yet, hidden though it was, he himself had held the tie-breaking vote. Perhaps the intensity of the inner dialogue had made it necessary for him to reassure himself of his own choice by pushing it to the edge and casting his vote over and over again. Each time he had survived he could feel once again his own wish to live. When the unconscious struggle is that intense, you might have to revisit the choice often through accidents and dangerous living just to be sure.

Cancer was only the last in a long series of crises which put the question of his life to the test. It was why he was here. But now that he had cancer it was going to be necessary to choose once and for all. Surviving life-threatening illness may require such a coherency between conscious and unconscious choice.

Max had metastatic colon cancer. The experts had given him daunting statistics and offered only a guarded prognosis. Yet expertise is not clairvoyance. As experts, we only deal with probability and not specific outcome. Like most people who do this sort of work, I have seen that the prognosis may not be the reality any more than the map is the territory or the blueprint, the building.

Max lived for eight years after this first meeting. We worked together for a few years exploring the doorway that had opened in this first session and I came to have a deep affection for this tough, funny, and very kind man. Gradually he became able to understand and forgive both his parents and to value and care for himself. His injuries and his accidents stopped. In the first few months he often joked about the moment when I cast my vote with him. "Outnumbered the bastard once and for all," he would chuckle.

When I told him that I wanted him to live, I spoke as a person to whom his life was important and not as someone who knew what his outcome would be. Under their expertise every physician feels this way about every patient, no matter what the odds. It is the motivation behind all that training, all that effort, the basis of all that commitment. I just think that sometimes it is important to say these sorts of things out loud.

A FRONT-ROW SEAT

IT IS HARD TO TRUST something you cannot see. Even after seven major surgeries, I have had at times difficulty in trusting my healing. In 1981, I developed peritonitis and sepsis when the sutures holding my intestine together gave way a few days after a six-hour abdominal surgery. By the time this was correctly diagnosed, I had become gravely ill. I was rushed back to the operating room, where further surgery probably saved my life. I remember being pushed down a corridor at a dead run, the lights overhead flashing by, my surgeon, who was also my friend, running alongside my gurney. Medical culture being what it is, he was talking to me about my case as if we were two physicians lunching in the doctors' dining room, talking about a mutual patient. "You know," he said conversationally, "because of the infection we will have to close by primary intention." Filled with drugs and very ill, I remember thinking, "Primary intention. I used to know what that means." Then events accelerated and I lost track of it all.

Several hours later, I awoke in the recovery room giddy with the realization that I had once again survived. Barely conscious, I explored my abdomen with a fingertip. There was the big soft bandage just as before. Comforted by the familiar, I drifted off.

The next day a nurse appeared to change my dressings. Chatting comfortably, she pulled back the bandages and I looked down expecting to see the usual fourteen-inch incision with its neat row of a hundred or more stitches. Instead, there was a great gaping wound, as open as any I'd ever seen while assisting in the operating room. My surgeon's words came back to me in a rush—*primary intention*—and today I knew what this meant. In the presence of infection there would be no sutures. The peritoneum and fascia would be closed and then the wound would be left open to heal on its own.

Deeply shocked, I looked down at the ruin of my abdomen. Surely this was a mortal wound. I remember thinking, "There is no way that such a thing can heal." The nurse chatted on cheerfully, unaware of my reaction. Taping the dressing back in place, she left the room. The next morning she was back to change the dressing again. This time I turned my head aside and wouldn't look. She spoke to me pleasantly while she performed her task. I didn't answer. I was in despair.

For several mornings, we went through this same routine, she pulling back the bandage, murmuring encouragement, I, head averted, awaiting the end. After a week or so, it occurred to me that against all probability, I was still here. Perhaps I would not die of this wound after all, but would have to live with it. This raised a completely different set of concerns and obsessions. How would I live with this great hole in my front? Perhaps after many years it might fill in and become flat—a scar fourteen inches long and several inches wide. Until then no tight jeans or bathing suits. Could I wear extra-large clothes? Or fill the deep trench in my belly with cotton and tape it in so it would not show?

After a few days of such musings, it became obvious that if I was going to live with it, I would need to see it. So that day, when the nurse pulled back the dressing, I forced myself to look again, expecting to see the gaping wound of ten days before. But it was not the same. Astounded, I saw that it had begun closing in at the bottom and was distinctly narrower. And then an extraordinary thing began to happen. Day after day, she would pull back the dressing and I would watch as this great wound, in the slow, patient way of all natural things, gradually became a hairline scar. And I, a physician, was not in control of this. It was humbling. Yet I certainly had a front-row seat at the healing process. It was only much later that I realized that I had been occupying this same front-row seat since the moment I had entered medical school. The life force I had witnessed in myself was a birthright common to us all.

STYLE

WHILE AN IMPULSE toward wholeness is natural and exists in everyone, each of us heals in our own way. Some people heal because they have work to do. Others heal because they have been released from their work and the pressures and expectations that others place on them. Some people need music, others need silence, some need people around them, others heal alone. Many different things can activate and strengthen the life force in us. For each of us there are conditions of healing that are as unique as a fingerprint. Sometimes people ask me what I do in my sessions with patients. Often I just remind people of the possibility of healing and study their own way of healing with them.

Some time ago a young man was referred to me by an imagery-training program for people with cancer. Despite a diagnosis of malignant melanoma, he had been so poorly motivated that only a month after completing the intensive training, he could not remember to do his daily imagery meditation. The referral had been clear; perhaps I could turn around his self-destructive tendencies and encourage him to fight for his life.

Jim was an air traffic controller at a major airport. He was a reserved and quiet man who might have been thought shy until you noticed the steadiness in his eyes. He told me with embarrassment that he was the only one in the imagery class who couldn't stick to the program. He didn't understand why. We talked for a while about his plans for his life and his reaction to his diagnosis. He certainly cared a great deal about getting well. He enjoyed his work, loved his family, looked forward to raising his little boy. Not much self-destruction there. So I asked him to tell me about his imagery.

By way of an answer he unfolded a drawing of a shark. The shark's mouth was huge and open and filled with sharp, pointed teeth. For fifteen minutes three times a day he was to imagine thousands of tiny sharks hunting through his body, savagely attacking and destroying any cancer cells they found. It was a fairly traditional pattern of immune system imagery, recommended by many self-help books and used by countless people. I asked him what seemed to prevent him from doing the meditation. With a sigh, he said he had found it boring.

The training had gone badly for him from the start. On the first day, the class had been asked to find an image for the immune system. In the subsequent discussion, he had discovered that he had not gotten the "right" sort of image. The whole class and the psychologist/leader had worked with him until he came up with this shark. I looked at the drawing on his lap. The contrast between it and this reserved man was striking.

Curious, I asked what his first image had been. Looking

away, he mumbled, "Not vicious enough." It had been a catfish. I was intrigued. I knew nothing about catfish, had never even seen one, and no one had ever talked about them in this healing role before. With growing enthusiasm he described what catfish do in an aquarium. Unlike other more aggressive and competitive fish, they are bottom feeders, sifting the sand through their gills, evaluating constantly, sorting waste from what is not waste, eating what no longer supports the life of the aquarium. They never sleep. They are able to make many rapid and accurate decisions. As an air traffic controller, he admired their ability to do this.

I asked him to describe catfish for me in a few words. He came up with such words as "discerning, vigilant, impeccable, thorough, steadfast." And "trustworthy." "Not bad," I thought.

We talked for a while about the immune system. He had not known that the DNA of each of our billions of cells carries a highly individual signature, a sort of personal designer logo. Our immune cells can recognize our own DNA logo and will consume any cell that does not carry it. The immune system is the defender of our identity on the cellular level, patrolling the Self/Not Self boundary constantly, discerning what is self from what is other, never sleeping. Cancer cells have lost their DNA logo. The healthy immune system attacks them and destroys them. In fact, his unconscious mind had offered him a particularly accurate image for the immune system.

As a medical student I had been involved in a study in which a micrograft, a tiny group of skin cells, was taken from one person and grafted onto the skin of a second person, and I told him of these experiments. In seventy-two hours, the second person's immune system, searching through the billions of cells that carried his own DNA signature, would find this tiny group of cells which carried the wrong DNA signature and destroy them. I described the many ingenious things we did to hide or conceal the micrograft. Try as we might, we could not outwit the immune system. It found those cells and destroyed them every time.

He still seemed doubtful. The teacher and the class had talked of the importance of an aggressive "fighting spirit" and of the "killer motivation" of effective cancer-fighting imagery. He flushed again. "Is there something else?" I asked him. Nodding, he told me that catfish grew big where he had been raised, and at certain times of the year they would "walk" across the roads. When he was a child this had struck him as a sort of miracle and he never tired of watching them. He had kept several as pets. "Jim," I said, "what is a pet?" He looked surprised. "Why, a pet is something that loves you, no matter what," he replied.

So I asked him to summarize his own imagery. Closing his eyes, he spoke of millions of catfish that never slept, moving through his body, vigilant, untiring, dedicated, and discriminating, patiently examining every cell, passing by the ones that were healthy, eating the ones that were cancerous, motivated by a pet's unconditional love and devotion. They cared whether he lived or died. He was as special and unique to them as he was to his dog. He opened his eyes. "This may sound silly but I feel sort of grateful to them for their care," he said.

This imagery touched him deeply and it was not hard for him to remember it. Nor was it boring. He did his meditation daily for a year. Years later, after a full recovery, he continues this practice a few times a week. He says it reminds him that, on the deepest level, his body is on his side.

People can learn to study their life force in the same way that a master gardener studies a rosebush. No gardener ever made a rose. When its needs are met a rosebush will make roses. Gardeners collaborate and provide conditions which favor this outcome. And as anyone who has ever pruned a rosebush knows, life flows through every rosebush in a slightly different way.

SILENCE

As an adolescent, I had a summer job working as a volunteer companion in a nursing home for the aged. The job began with a two-week intensive training about communicating with the elderly. There seemed to be a great deal to remember and what had begun as a rather heartfelt way to spend a teenage summer quickly became a regimented set of techniques and skills for which I would be evaluated by the nursing staff. By the first day of actual patient contact, I was very anxious.

My first assignment was to visit with a ninety-six-year-old woman who had not spoken for more than a year. A psychiatrist had diagnosed her as having senile dementia, but she had not responded to medication. The nurses doubted that she would talk to me, but hoped I could engage her in a mutual activity. I was given a large basket filled with glass beads of every imaginable size and color. We would string beads together. I was to report back to the nursing station in an hour.

I did not want to see this patient. Her great age frightened me and the words "senile dementia" suggested that not only was she older by far than anyone I had ever met, she was crazy, too. Filled with foreboding, I knocked on the closed door of her room. There was no answer. Opening the door, I found myself in a small room lit by a single window which faced the morning sun. Two chairs had been placed in front of the window; in one sat a very old lady, looking out. The other was empty. I stood just inside the door for a time, but she did not acknowledge my presence in any way. Uncertain of what to do next, I went to the empty chair and sat down, the basket of beads on my lap. She did not seem to notice that I had come.

For a while I tried to find some way to open a conversation. I was painfully shy at this time, which was one of the reasons my parents had suggested I take this job, and I would have had a hard time even in less difficult circumstances. The silence in the room was absolute. Somehow it almost seemed rude to speak, yet I desperately wanted to succeed in my task. I considered and discarded all the ways of making conversation suggested in the training. None of them seemed possible. The old woman continued to look toward the window, her face half hidden from me, barely breathing. Finally I simply gave up and sat with the basket of glass beads in my lap for the full hour. It was quite peaceful.

The silence was broken at last by the little bell which signified the end of the morning activity. Taking hold of the basket again, I prepared to leave. But I was only fourteen and curiosity overcame me. Turning to the old woman, I asked, "What are you looking at?" I immediately flushed. Prying into the lives of the residents was strictly forbidden. Perhaps she had not heard. But she had. Slowly she turned toward me and I could see her face for the first time. It was radiant. In a voice filled with joy she said, "Why, child, I am looking at the Light."

Many years later, as a pediatrician, I would watch newborns look at light with that same rapt expression, almost as if they were listening for something. Fortunately, I had not been able to find a way to interrupt.

A ninety-six-year-old woman may stop speaking because arteriosclerosis has damaged her brain, or she has become psychotic and she is no longer able to speak. But she may also have withdrawn into a space between the worlds, to contemplate what is next, to spread her sails and patiently wait to catch the light.

I had found her by accident, or perhaps by grace. I have often wondered what would have happened had I been the highly trained technical physician I would shortly become. At that time I would not have known how to find her and sit with her. How to learn from her about silence and trusting life. Now, many years later, I hope that I do.

READING BETWEEN THE LINES

SARA IS A WOMAN WHO, like myself, has had Crohn's disease for many years. In thirty years of illness she has had more than fourteen abdominal and joint surgeries. As a result of these experiences she saw herself as a victim. When she first came to my office, she was chronically depressed and incapacitated by self-pity. But over time that changed. Now she works three days a week and participates in the busy life of her family. When she completed her counseling sessions, her husband commented on the changes she had made and said it was like being married to another woman.

A year after I had last seen her she developed pain in her jaw and went to see her dentist. He diagnosed a small abscess in the bone and told her that she would need root canal surgery to correct it. As he began to describe the procedure, she abruptly stood and left his office. A few hours later I received an alarmed phone call from her husband, who had come home from work to find her sitting in her bathrobe in the living room, deeply depressed. He had no idea why, as she was unwilling to talk to him about it. "Come over," I said.

I was horrified by the change in Sara; she looked much as she had when we first met three years ago. Her eyes were lifeless, her hair uncombed. Her mismatched clothes seemed to be the first that had come to hand when she went to her closet. She sat slumped in the chair opposite me. In a flat voice, she told me what had happened in the dentist's office that afternoon. "It's just too much, I can't do it," she said. "This straw breaks the camel's back."

"What is going on, Sara?" I asked. She began to cry. "I don't know," she said. "I feel the same way I did when I first came here, sort of overwhelmed, beaten down." I suggested we try some of the imagery that had been so helpful to her before. Perhaps it would help her uncover the reason for her distress. In tears, she agreed.

I encouraged her to sit back in her chair and relax. Slowly she was able to follow the familiar pattern. When her breathing slowed and became a bit deeper I suggested that she imagine herself standing before a closed door. "When you feel ready, reach forward and open the door," I said. "On the other side you will find something that will help you with your feelings."

Opening this imaginary door, she was surprised to find herself in a hospital room. The patient in the bed was herself, in a coma, at the onset of her disease some thirty years ago.

Over the next fifteen minutes or so, she visited hospital

room after hospital room in her imagination. Slowly the events of her long illness began to unfold, year by year, operation by operation, setback after setback, recovery by recovery. As I went along with her, my logical mind began to object. Privately I wondered how any of this could possibly be of help to her now. Wouldn't revisiting all this pain cause her to feel even more victimized and helpless? Yet as she went on and on, her voice got stronger and she began to straighten up in her chair. She had just come to the year 1988 and was standing in an operating room watching what must have been her twelfth surgery, in which her right hip was completely replaced, when suddenly she opened her eyes and burst out laughing. "Root canal, schmoot canal," she howled, tears of laughter rolling down her face. "I can do this itty-bitty surgery with one hand tied behind my back."

By reviewing the story of her disease, Sara was able to experience the story behind the story, the personal meaning in the familiar facts and events. Looking deeply and honestly at her woundedness, she had found her power; experienced her own indomitable will to live, her courage, and her ability to heal herself over and over again. Perhaps every "victim" is really a survivor who does not know it yet.

DAMMING THE RIVER

AT THE BEGINNING, I reacted to suffering and limitation with rage. At fifteen, when I had become very ill, I needed to consult my disease on the simplest matters. Would it allow me to eat a piece of cheese? Did I have the strength to walk up this flight of stairs? Would it be possible to sit through the movies without needing to leave because of agonizing stomach pains? The authority of this disease would brook no argument from me. It still shapes my life, but with a far lighter hand.

Perhaps only an adolescent can feel the sort of rage I felt then. I hated all the well people, hated the side of my family that had passed me these genes. I hated my body. I was in this state of rage for almost ten years.

Shortly before my final year of medical training, things changed. I had been offered the opportunity to be senior resident at a fine training hospital. Yet I barely had enough strength to do the work I was presently doing. Here was one more dream stolen. That afternoon I drove to the old beach house that had been given to our hospital for the use of the faculty and staff. In turmoil, I walked wearily along the water's edge, comparing myself to others my own age, people of seemingly boundless vitality. I came up wanting. I remember thinking that this disease had robbed me of my youth. I did not yet know what it had given me in exchange.

In response to these painful thoughts, a wave of intense rage flooded me, the sort of feeling I had experienced many times before. But for some reason, this time I did not drown in it. Instead, I sort of noticed it go by and something inside me said, "You have no vitality? Here's your vitality."

Shocked, I recognized the connection between my anger and my will to live. My anger was my will to live turned inside out. My life force was just as intense, just as powerful as my anger, but for the first time I could experience it as different and feel it directly. In that first moment of surprise, I had a glimpse of something fundamental about who I am; that at the core of things I have an intense love of life, a wish to participate fully in life and to help others to do the same. Somehow this had grown large in me as a result of the very limitations that I had thought were thwarting it. Like the power of a dammed river. I had not known this before. I also knew that in its present form, as rage, this power was trapped. My anger had helped me to survive, to resist my disease, even to fight on, but in the form of anger I could not use my strength to build the kind of life I longed to live. And then I knew that I no longer needed to do it this way. I knew with absolute certainty that my pain was nobody's fault;

that the world was not to blame for it. It was a moment of real freedom.

I took that job. When things got rough, I asked others for their help. I had been too angry and bitter to do that before. It was a very important year.

Many years later, in a class on Aryuvedic medicine, I heard this sort of experience given a theoretical basis. Aryuveda suggests that there is a difference between energy and energy pattern or energy form, the container through which a person's life energy is flowing at any given moment. The shape of their energy, as it were. The energy form is anger or sorrow or joy or disappointment, but the energy itself is the chi, or the life force. In Chinese, the words for becoming angry, *shen qi,* mean "generating the chi," or increasing the life force.

I still get angry sometimes, but in ordinary ways. My anger does not begin to compare to the rage that was my life companion for all those years. That rage served me well. It defended my integrity. It said no to the limitations of my disease. But something else would be required to say yes to my life.

II.
Judgment

THE LIFE IN US is diminished by judgment far more frequently than by disease. Our own self-judgment or the judgment of other people can stifle our life force, its spontaneity and natural expression. Unfortunately, judgment is commonplace. It is as rare to find someone who loves us as we are as it is to find someone who loves themselves whole.

Judgment does not only take the form of criticism. Approval is also a form of judgment. When we approve of people, we sit in judgment of them as surely as when we criticize them. Positive judgment hurts less acutely than criticism, but it is judgment all the same and we are harmed by it in far more subtle ways. To seek approval is to have no resting place, no sanctuary. Like all judgment, approval encourages a constant striving. It makes us uncertain of who we are and of our true value. This is as true of the approval we give ourselves as it is of the approval we offer others. Approval can't be trusted. It can be withdrawn at any time no matter what our track record has been. It is as nourishing of real growth as cotton candy. Yet many of us spend our lives pursuing it.

Some people spend enormous amounts of time considering the impression that their words and behaviors create, checking how their performance will affect their audience, playing always for approval. Others make a tiny gap between their thoughts and their words which allows them to say only that which they feel will please others. A great deal of energy goes into this process of fixing and editing ourselves. We may have even come to admire in ourselves what is admired, expect what is expected, and value what is valued by others. We have changed ourselves into someone that the people who matter to us can love. Sometimes we no longer know what is true for us, in which direction our own integrity lies.

We surrender our wholeness for a variety of reasons. Among the most compelling are our ideas of what being a good person is all about. Sometimes it is not the approval of other people but the approval of a spiritual school or teacher which dictates which parts of us we keep and which we hide. The natural self, a complex living interchange of seemingly opposite characteristics, gets whittled down against some acquired standard of social and spiritual acceptability. Few of us are able to love ourselves as we are. We may even have become ashamed of our wholeness.

Parts of ourselves which we may have hidden all of our lives out of shame are often the source of our healing. We have all been taught that certain of our ways don't fit into the common viewpoint and values of the society or the family into which we have been born. Every culture, every family has its Shadow. When we're told that "big boys don't cry," and "ladies never disagree with anyone," we learn to avoid judgment by disowning our feelings and our perspectives. We make ourselves less whole. It is only human to trade wholeness for approval. Yet parts we disown are not lost, they are just forgotten. We can remember our wholeness at any time. In hiding it, we have kept it safe.

One of the most dramatic manifestations of the life force is seen in the plant kingdom. When times are harsh and what is needed to bloom cannot be found, certain plants become spores. These plants dampen down and wall off their life force in order to survive. It is an effective strategy. Spores found in mummies, spores thousands of years old, have unfolded into plants when given the opportunity of nurture.

When no one listens, children form spores. In an environment hostile to their uniqueness, when they are judged, criticized, and reshaped through approval into what is wanted rather than supported and allowed to develop naturally into who they are, children wall the unloved parts of themselves away. People may become spores young and stay that way throughout most of their lives. But a spore is a survival strategy, not a way of life. Spores do not grow. They endure. What you needed to do to survive may be very different from what you need to do to live.

Plant spores are opportunists. The life force waits in them, scanning the environment, looking for the first opportunity to bloom. But people may forget that becoming a spore is only a temporary strategy. Few check the environment, as plant spores do, to see if conditions have changed and they can find what they need to bloom and reclaim their wholeness. Many of us still hide the parts of ourselves that were unacceptable to our parents and teachers although our parents are long gone and their world with them. In the world of my childhood, boys never cried. Those that did were sissies. Of course, all girls were supposed to be sissies. The world we live in now offers far greater opportunities for expression, but we may still live in it as if it were the hostile terrain of our childhood. The saddest part is that we may have forgotten what it is like to be whole. What it is like to feel and to cry, what it is like to take initiative and have a viewpoint.

Reclaiming ourselves usually means coming to recognize and accept that we have in us both sides of everything. We are capable of fear and courage, generosity and selfishness, vulnerability and strength. These things do not cancel each other out but offer us a full range of power and response to life. Life is as complex as we are. Sometimes our vulnerability is our strength, our fear develops our courage, and our woundedness is the road to our integrity. It is not an either/or world. It is a real world. In calling ourselves "heads" or "tails," we may never own and spend our human currency, the pure gold of which our coin is made.

But judgment may heal over time. One of the blessings of growing older is the discovery that many of the things I once believed to be my shortcomings have turned out in the long run to be my strengths, and other things of which I was unduly proud have revealed themselves in the end to be among my shortcomings. Things that I have hidden from others for years turn out to be the anchor and enrichment of my middle age. What a blessing it is to outlive your self-judgments and harvest your failures.

GETTING IT RIGHT

I HAD FIRST MET George when he was a fourth-year student at Berkeley, the year his father had been diagnosed with prostate cancer. Now in his final year of graduate school, he had come back because of problems that he did not feel he could discuss elsewhere. When his dad had been ill his housemate Michael had been his greatest support. Now Michael was in trouble, traveling in a hard-partying crowd that used cocaine socially. George felt that Michael was becoming addicted. All his tactful efforts to discuss this possibility went unheard. Michael's brilliance more than compensated for his habit and he continued to do so well at school that no one but George suspected his problem.

George was a serious practitioner of Buddhism. As he understood it, the core of this spiritual teaching is a position of nonjudgment and noninterference. This did not come easily to George. His family routinely criticized each other and told each other how to live. Holding what he took to be a Buddhist position toward Michael got even harder for him as Michael became more and more erratic in his personal behavior. George was uncertain what to do and so he had come to sort things out.

Their relationship reached a crisis point one evening when George brought home a young woman whose opinion mattered a great deal to him. Opening the front door, he was stunned to find Michael shirtless and dazed, sprawled on the living room floor. He had vomited on himself.

"I looked at the expression on Liz's face and I just lost it," George told me ruefully. "I picked Michael up, pushed him into the bathroom, turned on the shower and shoved him into it. I remember standing there with the cold water pouring down on both of us, slamming him against the wall and shouting the most terrible things. I called him names. I told him all the things I had struggled for months not to think and feel. And then I gave him an ultimatum—clean up or get out. It was just too hard to watch him throw himself away and I was not going to do it. When he seemed awake, I changed my wet clothes, and went home with Liz."

In the morning, George was contrite and disheartened. Ten years of Buddhist practice and he had reacted exactly as his own father would have reacted. He had failed to meet his own standards of compassion. He had judged Michael harshly and he was bitterly disappointed in himself. He dreaded going back to the apartment. Maybe Michael would not be there.

But Michael *was* there. Pale and obviously unwell, but straight, Michael was sitting on the couch waiting. They talked. George heard about things he had not known. How Michael, the only child of a socially prominent and wealthy family, had been raised by paid strangers and sent away to boarding school at seven. How he had been sent away to camp during the summers. How he had been given anything he wanted but no one had thought him worth their time or attention. No one had ever cared what he did with himself the way that George seemed to care last night.

In the shower Michael had understood that his life mattered to George, that what he was doing was causing George pain. Quietly he told George that he knew he was in trouble, had known it for months, but hadn't thought that anyone would care to help, would spend the time to help. "Would you help me, George?" he asked, and began to cry.

This all happened some years ago and the story has a happy ending. For a year, the two went nightly to a cocaine addiction program. It wasn't easy but together they were successful. Michael is now a well-established businessman with a loving wife and a small child. George, in reflecting back on this time, feels that it was a major learning experience for him.

"I was always trying to get it right. Between Buddhism and business school I was always working on myself, my reactions, and my feelings to meet some standard of excellence. Somehow, it had never occurred to me that who I really was could be all right. If God had wanted Michael to live with Buddha he would have given him Buddha for a roommate. Instead he gave him a caring middle-class guy from a traditional midwestern family whose parents had never even been drunk. When I finally acted from my integrity, I was just what was needed. In the end, all I had to give to Michael was my integrity. And it was enough."

MEETING MR. RIGHT

DURING A LONG AGO trip to Canada, I visited a historic graveyard and came across a headstone inscribed: "Here lies George Brown, born a man, died a gastroenterologist." I could not have been more than twelve or thirteen at the time and I remember being inspired by this. Since medical expertise was so highly respected in my family, I had thought this was a step up. I am no longer as inspired by expertise as I once was. Perhaps the worth of any lifetime is measured more in kindness than in competency.

One of my former clients is a psychologist and a fine athlete who ran every morning in a park near her home before going to her office. She often met a colleague there, a well-known psychiatrist. Without any formal arrangement, they had run together at about the same time for many years. After she was diagnosed with cancer, somehow her running companion was never there. My client is a strong and determined woman and despite a difficult course of surgery and chemotherapy, she continued to run every day. After a few months of running alone, she called the psychiatrist at his office, but he never returned the call.

About a year after the completion of her chemotherapy she took a different path one morning and saw the psychiatrist running up ahead. Being twenty years younger, she overtook him easily. As they ran side by side, she told her old running companion that it had hurt when he had not called back. The professional community they both belonged to was small and almost everyone had known about her cancer. Surely he had heard. The psychiatrist's answer had shocked her. He had replied, "I'm sorry. I simply did not know the right thing to say."

I asked her what she would have wanted to hear. She smiled sadly. "Oh, something like, 'I heard it's been a hard year. How are you doing?' Some simple human thing like that."

BACK TO BASICS

SEVERAL YEARS AGO, I was invited to give a talk about my work with people with cancer to a group of women physicians at a local meeting of the American Women's Medical Association. In the discussion after the talk, an internist commented that she would find this work difficult. She had avoided caring for people with cancer because a certain percentage of them would die and she found it upsetting to care for dying patients. "I hate it when I've run out of treatments, when there is nothing more I can do," she confessed. Others in the group nodded their agreement.

I asked them when they first became uncomfortable in these situations. The women were surprised to notice that they had not been as uncomfortable before medical school. As the discussion went on, it became clearer that we were more uncomfortable in these situations as doctors than as women. As women, we knew there was something simple and natural in just being there, together. Slowly some insights emerged. Women have always been present at these times, at death and birth and in many of the other transitions in life. Women have gathered at the transitions, as comforters and companions, as witnesses, to mark the importance of the moment.

One of the physicians talked about caring for her dying mother when she was nineteen years old. She had expected a great deal less of herself then. At first she had driven her mother to her doctor's appointments, shopped for food, and run errands. As her mother grew weaker, she had prepared tempting meals and cleaned the house. When her mother stopped eating, she had listened to her and read to her for hours. When her mother slipped into coma, she had changed her sheets, bathed her, and rubbed her back with lotion. There always seemed to be something more to do. A way to care. These ways became simpler and simpler. "In the end," she told us, "I just held her and sang."

There was a long, thoughtful silence. Then one of the older women said that she too had tended to avoid situations when there were no treatments left. She had felt powerless. But she saw now that even when there was nothing left to do *medically,* there were still other things she could say or do that might matter. Kind things. Ways she could still be of help. She had simply forgotten. Her voice wavered slightly.

I looked at her more closely. This tough and competent sixty-year-old surgeon had tears in her eyes. It was quite amazing.

BEYOND PERFECTION

WHOLENESS LIES beyond perfection. Perfection is only an idea. For most experts and many of the rest of us it has become a life goal. The pursuit of perfection may actually be dangerous to your health. The Type A personality for whom perfectionism is a way of life is associated with heart disease. Perfectionism can break your heart and all the hearts around you.

A perfectionist sees life as if it were one of those little pictures that used to appear in the newspapers over the caption "What's wrong with this picture?" If you looked at the picture carefully you would see that the table only had three legs or the house had no door. I remember the "Aha!" that these pictures evoked in me as a child. I wonder now why anyone would want to take such satisfaction in seeing what is missing, what is wrong, what is "broken."

The pursuit of perfection has become a major addiction of

our time. Fortunately, perfectionism is learned. No one is born a perfectionist, which is why it is possible to recover. I am a recovering perfectionist. Before I began recovering, I experienced that I and everyone else was always falling short, that who we were and what we did was never quite good enough. I sat in judgment on life itself. Perfectionism is the belief that life is broken.

Sometimes perfectionists have had a parent who is a perfectionist, someone who awarded approval on the basis of performance and achievement. Children can learn early that they are loved for what they do and not simply for who they are. To a perfectionistic parent, what you do never seems as good as what you might do if you tried just a little harder. The life of such children can become a constant striving to earn love. Of course love is never earned. It is a grace we give one another. Anything we need to earn is only approval.

Few perfectionists can tell the difference between love and approval. Perfectionism is so widespread in this culture that we actually have had to invent another word for love. "Unconditional love," we say. Yet, all love is unconditional. Anything else is just approval.

The pursuit of perfection is built into every professional training. But long before I went to medical school, I was trained as a perfectionist by my father. As a child, when I brought home a ninety-eight on an exam, he invariably responded, "What happened to the other two points?"

I adored my dad, and my whole childhood was focused on the pursuit of the other two points. By the time I was in my twenties, I had become as much a perfectionist as he. It was no longer necessary for him to ask me about those two points: I had taken that over for myself. It was many years before I found out that those points don't matter. That they are not the secret to living a life worth remembering. That they don't make you lovable. Or whole.

Life offers us many teachers and many teachings. One of mine was David, who was an artist and my first love. The living proof that opposites attract. While we were together, my driver's license came up for renewal. And I needed to take a written test of the traffic laws.

The DMV had sent a little booklet. I studied it for days. All the while I was memorizing the meaning of the white curb and the yellow curb, David would try to persuade me to join him for a walk or go to a party or out to dinner or dancing or even just talk. I told him I couldn't take the time. Of course I got 100% on the test. Triumphant, I rushed into his studio shouting that I had gotten 100% on my driving test. David looked up from his painting with an expression of great tenderness. "My love," he said, "why would you want to do that?"

It was not the response I had expected. Suddenly I understood that I had sacrificed a great deal to get a hundred on a test that I had only needed to pass in order to drive. I had spent days studying for it that I could have spent in much wiser ways. I had learned many things that I did not even want to know. It had felt as if I had no choice. If my father could not approve of me with anything less than 100, I could not approve of myself with less than 100 either. Even on a written driving test. Like most addicts, I was out of control.

It was clearly not about driving. It was not even about grades. It was about needing to deserve love. Fortunately, David did not play by these rules. He didn't even know the game.

THE ORDINARY HERO

My uncle was a hero. Like all of the men in my mother's family, he was a physician, a general practitioner and later a pathologist. During World War II, he was caught up in an action for which he received a medal.

The story went like this: My uncle was one of a group of physicians following the troops. Acting on false information, the soldiers pressed forward believing the ridge on which they were advancing had been cleared of enemy fire. As they moved out of cover, the hidden enemy opened fire and within seconds the field was covered with wounded and dying men. The enemy continued to blanket the area with live fire. No one could stand upright. It was more than twelve hours before air reinforcements could cripple the enemy position. My uncle, crawling on his belly with supplies strapped to his back, placed tourniquets, stopped bleeding, took messages sometimes written on the back of worn photographs, and gave last rites, during all that time.

When reinforcements came and the enemy was pulled back it was clear that he had saved dozens of lives.

He was decorated for this action and his picture was on the front page of our hometown newspaper, the *New York Daily Mirror.* I was about seven at the time, and with a real hero in my family, I instantly became the talk of the second grade. Best of all, he had been given leave and was coming to visit us. I was giddy with excitement.

Secretly, I was surprised by these events. My uncle was short, balding, and wore glasses. He even had a little potbelly. Perhaps he would look different now. But he didn't. Always a shy man, he seemed uncomfortable with all the fuss and uneasy as neighbor after neighbor came by to shake his hand. Finally I found my moment. Climbing into his lap, I told him how brave I thought he was and that I was sure he was never afraid of anything. Smiling, he told me that this was far from the case, that he had been more frightened than ever before in his life. Severely disappointed, I blurted out, "But why did they give you a medal then?"

Gently he explained to me that anyone who wasn't afraid in situations like war was a fool and they don't give medals to people for being fools. That being brave does not mean being unafraid. It often means being afraid and doing it anyway.

It was the first of the many teachings about courage I have received in my lifetime and it meant a great deal to me. At the time, I was afraid of the dark and deeply ashamed about this. But if my uncle who was a hero was also afraid, then perhaps there was hope for me as well. I had been stopped by my fear, humiliated by it, wounded in my sense of self. By telling me of his fear, my uncle had freed me. His heroism became a part of my story as well as a part of his.

PROFESSIONALS DON'T CRY

ONE OF THE MOST common experiences in the practice of medicine is the experience of loss and disappointment. Physicians typically experience many disappointments every week, from the small nudge of the lab test revealing that a medication is not effective, to the blow of a patient dying. It is a great deal for any caring person to handle. Yet most of this loss remains unacknowledged and ungrieved.

I teach a course now at our local medical school to the first- and second-year students. In one of the evening seminars, we explore our attitudes toward loss, uncover some of the beliefs about loss we inherited from our families, identify our habitual strategies for dealing with loss, and examine what we do instead of grieving. This is often a rich and deeply moving experience which allows the students to know themselves and each other in different ways.

At the close of one of these evenings, a woman student stood and told me that her class had already been given two lectures on grieving by the department of psychiatry. I had not known this and I apologized, saying that it might have been better to choose another topic for the evening's discussion. "Oh no," she said, "it was different. They taught us grief theory and how to recognize when our patients are grieving a loss. And be respectful of that. They just didn't say that *we* would have anything to grieve."

The expectation that we can be immersed in suffering and loss daily and not be touched by it is as unrealistic as expecting to be able to walk through water without getting wet. This sort of denial is no small matter. The way we deal with loss shapes our capacity to be present to life more than anything else. The way we protect ourselves from loss may be the way in which we distance ourselves from life.

Protecting ourselves from loss rather than grieving and healing our losses is one of the major causes of burnout. Very few of the professionals I have treated for burnout actually came in saying that they were burned out. I don't think most of them knew. The most common thing I've been told is, "There's something wrong with me. I don't care anymore. Terrible things happen in front of me and I feel nothing."

Yet people who really don't care are rarely vulnerable to burnout. Psychopaths don't burn out. There are no burned-out tyrants or dictators. Only people who do care can get to this place of numbness. We burn out not because we don't care but because we don't grieve. We burn out because we have allowed our hearts to become so filled with loss that we have no room left to care.

The burnout literature talks about the factors which heal burnout: rest, exercise, play, the releasing of unrealistic expectations. In my experience burnout only really begins to heal when people learn how to grieve. Grieving is a way of self-care, the antidote to professionalism. Health professionals don't cry. Unfortunately.

The second day of my internship in pediatrics I went with my senior resident to tell some young parents that the automobile accident from which they had escaped without a scratch had killed their only child. Very new to this doctor thing, when they cried, I had cried with them. After it was over, the senior resident took me aside and told me that I had behaved very unprofessionally. "These people were counting on our strength," he said. I had let them down. I took his criticism very much to heart. By the time I myself was senior resident, I hadn't cried in years.

During that year a two-year-old baby, left unattended for only a moment, drowned in a bathtub. We fought to bring him back but after an hour we had to concede defeat. Taking the intern with me, I went to tell these parents that we had not been able to save their child. Overwhelmed, they began to sob. After a time, the father looked at me standing there, strong and silent in my white coat, the shaken intern by my side. "I'm sorry, Doctor," he said. "I'll get ahold of myself in a minute." I remember this man, his face wet with a father's tears, and I think of his apology with shame. Convinced by then that my grief was a useless, self-indulgent waste of time, I had made myself into the sort of a person to whom one could apologize for being in pain.

I remember a rotation on the pediatric service of Memorial Sloan-Kettering Cancer Center in New York. During this rotation we were actually losing a child a day. Every morning we would begin rounds in the autopsy room, talking to the pathologist about the child who died the day before or who was lost during the night, and every morning I would leave the autopsy room and go back to the children's ward telling myself, "Well, on to the next."

This attitude which was so prevalent in my training also happened to be the approach to loss I had learned in my family. The afternoon my ten-week-old kitten was run over, my mother took me to a pet store and bought me another. I was taught at a very early age that if something painful happened, the best thing to do was not to think about it and to get involved with something else. Unfortunately in medicine, the "something else" I got involved with was often another tragedy.

The bottom line is that grieving is not meant to be of help to any particular patient. You grieve because it's of help to you. It enables you to go forward after loss. It heals you so that you are able to love again. "On to the next" is a denial of a common humanity, an assertion that someone can die in front of us without touching us. It is a rejection of wholeness, of a human connection that is fundamental. It makes no sense at all when you say it out loud.

WHO IS THAT MASKED MAN?

AT ONE POINT two surgeons who were respected faculty at a nearby medical school were both patients of mine in my counseling practice. Each had come because of loneliness, depression, and burnout. Neither was aware that the other was also here seeking help.

As time went by, both men talked to me about the deep caring they felt they could not show to their patients or speak of to other physicians. Sometimes when things did not go well in the operating room or they lost a patient, they would share their feelings. Like myself, both of these men were trained to consider such behavior unprofessional, even unmanly. They felt alone with these emotions and isolated from other physicians because of them.

In the safety of my office they would also allow themselves

the freedom to wonder aloud about things that were beyond proof. Was there something more mysterious, less scientific that explained why some surgeons got better results than others? Were there unknown factors that promoted survival? They would muse about the will to live and worry about operating on patients who believed they were going to die. They would share stories about their patients with me, marveling at the strength with which people recovered or learned to live well despite terrible loss.

These two men had been professional partners for more than twenty years. They shared a receptionist, a staff of nurses, an office, but they didn't know each other. They shared a therapist, too, but I was ethically bound not to tell either about the other's visits or even that they were both my patients. I would encourage each of them to talk to his partner about these things, but I'd get the same response every time: "Him? Heavens, he would just laugh."

Like people with cancer, physicians often feel isolated from others by the nature of their experiences. They are also isolated from each other by the codes of professionalism. In the physician-training workshops I facilitate, loneliness becomes apparent in many different ways. During one of the sessions, a gastroenterologist talked of the unexpected death of one of his patients. Although it had happened years ago the pain was still acute and in the circle of physicians he began to cry. The others were very moved. Afterwards he told us that he had never cried about it before and he felt a great deal better. One of the others asked him why he had not cried. He said that it had seemed to him to be the sort of thing that only another physician could understand.

"And who would cry in front of another physician?" We all understood instantly.

Loneliness often emerges symbolically in these workshops as well. When asked to create a sand tray about his role as a physician, Jon, an oncological surgeon, constructed the following scene in the sand. Farthest away from himself he placed the open jaws of a shark. Between this and himself he placed a group of small clay figures in a circle. Among these figures there was a man bowed down in despair, a woman with one breast, on her knees with her arms upflung in prayer, another woman trying to hide with her hands the big hole where her heart should be, and a man with arms outstretched to ward off some unseen disaster. In the center of these figures he put a bit of burning incense, saying that its smoke represented the healing that was happening among these wounded people because they had each other.

Closest to himself he placed a kachina doll, in the Native American tradition a carved representation of an aspect of the spirit of healing. Interestingly, over time, several physicians in different study groups have selected this same figure to represent themselves. Hundreds of people with cancer have used these same sand tray objects. They also use this figure, but most commonly they use it to represent healing. The doctors' choice of this particular sand tray figure is especially significant because it is cracked and broken.

Jon placed a paper surgical mask in the sand between the kachina and the circle of figures, hiding the doll from their view. From behind the mask the doll had an unobstructed view only of the shark. I wondered if he had meant to show us so graphically the position from which he did his work. As he confronts cancer, his wounded self is isolated and invisible; the people he serves see only his surgical mask. His only clear view is of the disease. It was a poignant tray.

When asked to describe the meaning of what he had done, he offered the following interpretation: "There is threat," he said, pointing to the shark. "These figures are wounded people. My patients. In their midst is a place of healing. And here I am. Behind my surgical mask I am wounded also. I am missing my left ear. Behind my skills, my knowledge, I am hiding. Only the shark can see me; it knows I am here." When asked to find a word that summarized his tray he said, "Alone."

At the close of this exercise, people have an opportunity to make any changes they wish in their own tray. Jon moved the broken kachina doll from behind the surgical mask and placed it in the circle of other wounded figures. His eyes grew red but he did not cry.

The other physicians, watching, were visibly affected by Jon's contribution to the sand tray exercise. Afterwards they discussed it for hours. Others had felt as lonely but they had not been able to speak of it before.

KISSING THE BOO-BOO

We have been taught since childhood that pain is "poor form" and often react to it almost as if it is a breach of good manners. In other cultures, pain and loss are not as lonely. Facing loss alone makes us even more vulnerable and causes unnecessary suffering.

A new client came in after missing an appointment and told me that she had been in the emergency room the week before at the time she was supposed to be here in the office. I had not known this and I asked her what had happened. She told me that she had suffered a temporary obstruction of her bowel from adhesions caused by the radiation used to treat her cancer years ago. The pain had been severe and lasted for a day, but now it was over. When the pain began, she had recognized it as something of significance. She had packed a small bag, putting in her makeup, a nightie, and a mystery she was in the middle of reading. Then she had driven herself twenty-five miles to the hospital.

Having had several intestinal obstructions myself, I knew how severe such pain could be. I asked her how she had managed to drive. She told me that she had driven until the pain came, then she had pulled off the road and waited for it to pass. She had thought to bring a pot and a towel with her and once or twice she had vomited. She had been very sick but she had gotten to the hospital. It had taken a long time. Surprised, I asked her why she had not called a friend. She told me it was the middle of the day and everyone was working.

She had spent the next day in the emergency room alone. I asked her why she hadn't called anyone even then. "Why would I call anyone?" she responded with irritation. "None of my friends know a thing about intestinal obstruction."

"Then why didn't you call me?"

"Well, it's not really your field either," she replied.

"Jessie," I said, "even children instinctively run to others when they fall down." With a great deal of heat she said, "Yes, I've never understood that. It's so silly. Kissing the boo-boo doesn't help the pain at all." I was stunned. "Jessie," I said, "it doesn't help the pain, it helps the loneliness."

Many people deal with pain like Jessie did. When Jessie was in pain the only thing of value that another person could offer her was their expertise. Her mother had died when she was born. It had never occurred to her that anything could be done about the loneliness.

HOW IT WAS

As a pediatric intern, I was a secret baby kisser. This was so flagrantly "unprofessional" I was careful not to be discovered. Late at night under the guise of checking a surgical dressing or an IV, I would make solo rounds on the ward and kiss the children good night. If there was a favorite toy or blanket, I would be sure it was close, and if someone was crying I would even sing a little. I never mentioned this dimension of my health care to anyone. I felt the other residents, mostly men, might think less of me for it.

One evening as I was talking to a patient's father in the corridor, I glanced over his shoulder and saw Stan, my chief resident, bend over the crib of a little girl with leukemia and kiss her on the forehead. In that moment, I realized that others too might be struggling to extend themselves beyond an accepted professionalism to express a natural caring. Perhaps there was a way to talk about these things, even to support one another.

One night when we were waiting to be called to the operating room for a C-section, I told Stan what I had seen and that it had meant something important to me. Although we were alone in the doctors' lounge, Stan denied the whole thing.

We dropped the subject in embarrassment. For the rest of the year we worked together, thirty-six hours on call and twelve hours off. We became trusted colleagues, good friends, and even occasional drinking buddies, but we never mentioned the incident again.

Stan's integrity was almost legendary. He would never have fudged a piece of lab data or said he had read an article when he hadn't. But he would have had to step past our entire professional image and training to admit his heartfelt reaction to that little girl. It was impossible then. It is barely possible now. Expressing caring directly rather than through a willingness to work a thirty-six-hour day or spend long evenings keeping up with the medical literature and the newest treatments transgresses a strong professional code. It was just not professional behavior. I stopped kissing the babies then. It did not seem worth the risk.

In some ways, a medical training is like a disease. It would be years before I would fully recover from mine.

THE GIFT OF HEALING

THE COMMONWEAL CANCER HELP PROGRAM is a retreat for people with cancer in Northern California. Since the beginning of the program in 1984 we have held seventy-five week-long retreats. Every morning during the retreat, there is a discussion session which usually begins with a brief period of meditation. On one of the earliest retreats, Dieter was the first to speak after the silence. In his soft, deep voice he told us how important it was to him to be together with other people who had cancer, people who could understand how it was for him. He was silent for a while and then he started talking about his doctor, an oncologist, who had been giving him chemotherapy for some time.

Every week he would go to the doctor's office for his injection. Afterwards he and his doctor would sit together and talk quietly for a while. Fifteen minutes, no more. Until he came to Commonweal his doctor was the only person to whom he could talk honestly, who understood the experiences that he was going through.

Cancer had changed his life. He now lived so far beyond the usual, the normal, the ordinary in life, that he often felt alone. Many people did not want to hear about how it was with him, or couldn't understand things that had never happened to them. Some were so upset by the pain of it all that he felt the need to protect them from it through his silence. But his doctor understood. For fifteen minutes every week he was able to talk to somebody who listened, who didn't need him to explain, who was not afraid.

Dieter's life had been different even before his cancer. Born and raised in East Germany, he had escaped across the "no-man's-land," leaving behind him all that was familiar and dear. For years he had felt isolated and homeless, a refugee. Then he had met Lila, an American, who gathered him in and helped him belong again with her love. Shortly after he married her, he had been diagnosed with liver cancer.

For some time now Dieter had suspected that the chemotherapy was no longer helping him. Convinced at last of this, he spoke to his doctor and suggested that the treatments be stopped. He asked if he could come every week just to talk. His doctor responded abruptly. "If you refuse chemotherapy, there is nothing more I can do for you," he said.

Dieter had felt closed out and pushed away. "When I talk about not doing more chemotherapy, my doctor becomes all business. We are usually friends, but when I mention this his friendship cuts off. He is the one I talk to. His friendship means a lot to me." And so Dieter had continued to take the weekly injection in order to have those few moments of connection and understanding with his doctor.

The group of people with cancer listened intently. There was another silence, then Dieter said softly, "My doctor's love is as important to me as his chemotherapy, but he does not know."

Dieter's statement meant a great deal to me. I had not known, either. For a long time, I had carried the belief that as a physician my love didn't matter and the only thing of value I had to offer was my knowledge and skill. My training had argued me out of my truth. Medicine is as close to love as it is to science, and its relationships matter even at the edge of life itself.

But I had yet another connection to Dieter's story: his oncologist was one of my patients. Week after week, from the depths of a chronic depression this physician would tell me that no one cared about him, he didn't matter to anyone, he was just another white coat in the hospital, a mortgage payment to his wife, a tuition check to his son. No one would notice if he vanished as long as someone was there to make rounds or take out the garbage. So here is Dieter, bringing the same validation, the same healing to his doctor that he brought to me, but his doctor, caught up in a sense of failure because he cannot cure the cancer, cannot receive it.

ON NAMING AND AWE

A LABEL IS A MASK life wears.

We put labels on life all the time. "Right," "wrong," "success," "failure," "lucky," "unlucky," may be as limiting a way of seeing things as "diabetic," "epileptic," "manic-depressive," or even "invalid." Labeling sets up an expectation of life that is often so compelling we can no longer see things as they really are. This expectation often gives us a false sense of familiarity toward something that is really new and unprecedented. We are in relationship with our expectations and not with life itself.

Which brings up the idea that we may become as wounded by the way in which we see an illness as by the illness itself. Belief traps or frees us. Labels may become self-fulfilling prophecies. Studies of voodoo death suggest that in certain circumstances belief may even kill.

We may need to take our labels and even our experts far

more lightly. Some years ago I served on the dissertation committee of a woman in the Midwest, who was studying spontaneous remission of cancer. Among the people who answered her ad in the paper asking for people who thought they may have had an unusual experience of healing was a farmer who had done exceptionally well despite a dire prognosis. On the phone one evening, she told me about him. She felt his outcome was related to his attitude. "He didn't take it on," she said.

Confused, I asked her if he had denied that he had cancer. No, she said, he had not. He had just taken the same attitude toward his physician's prognosis that he took toward the words of the government soil experts who analyzed his fields. As they were educated men, he respected them and listened carefully as they showed him the findings of their tests and told him that the corn would not grow in this field. He valued their opinions. But, as he told my student, "A lot of the time the corn grows anyway."

In my experience, a diagnosis is an opinion and not a prediction. What would it be like if more people allowed for the presence of the unknown, and accepted the words of their medical experts in this same way? The diagnosis is cancer. What that will mean remains to be seen.

Like a diagnosis, a label is an attempt to assert control and manage uncertainty. It may allow us the security and comfort of a mental closure and encourage us not to think about things again. But life never comes to a closure, life is process, even mystery. Life is known only by those who have found a way to be comfortable with change and the unknown. Given the nature of life, there may be no security, but only adventure.

GRIST FOR THE MILL

ONE OF THE book agents responsible for getting many of the most innovative thinkers in psychology and spirituality published in the sixties and early seventies, years before anyone else could have sold these books, seemed to be a self-absorbed and ruthless man. At the time I met him I was studying spiritual paths, many of which emphasized the need to clean up your act in order to be able to serve a universal purpose. Yet here was a man to whom most spiritual teachers would have assigned a million years of practice, who had nevertheless done great good in the world, spreading life-affirming ideas through the culture like a Johnny Appleseed. But many spiritual schools would have encouraged people with the same personal traits to spend most of their time in meditation, preparing to serve. I just could not understand it.

Over the years I have learned that "cleaning up one's act"

may be far less important than consecrating one's life. It may be possible to use everything. A ruthless man may be able to open doors that a more kindly and traditionally spiritual person could knock on forever. Without judgment, many things can be made holy.

THE WOOD-OF-NO-NAMES

JUST BEFORE she meets with Tweedledum and Tweedledee, Alice enters the wood-of-no-names and encounters a fawn. Neither the fawn nor Alice can remember their names. No matter. They walk a ways together, "Alice with her arms clasped lovingly around the soft neck of the Fawn," until they come to the edge of the wood. Once there, the fawn suddenly remembers its name and looks at Alice with horror. "I'm a Fawn!" it cries out, "and, dear me! you're a human child!" Terrified, it runs away.

As a child I spent many summers alone on a deserted beach on Long Island, gathering shells, digging for little clams, leading a far different life than the city life I led the rest of the year. Day after day I watched everything, developing an eye for change in all its subtlety. The rest of the year in New York City, I did not look directly at anyone I did not know and did not talk to strangers.

There was great peace in those summers and a new ability to be without people and yet not alone. I have many good memories of that time. Every morning the sea would wash up new treasures—pieces of wood from sunken boats, bits of glass worn smooth as silk, the occasional jellyfish. Once I even found a pair of glasses with only one lens left in them. Some of the most vivid of these memories concerned the beautiful white birds that flew constantly overhead. I remember how their wings would become transparent when they passed between me and the sun. Angel wings. I remember how my heart followed them and how much I too wanted wings to fly.

Many years later I had the opportunity to walk this same beach. It was a great disappointment. Bits of seaweed and garbage littered the shoreline, and there were sea gulls everywhere, screaming raucously, fighting over the garbage and the occasional dead creature the sea had given up.

Disheartened, I drove home and was halfway there before I realized that the gulls were the white birds of my childhood. The beach had not changed. The sacred lives beyond labels and judgment, in the wood-of-no-names.

III.

Traps

THOSE WHO DON'T love themselves as they are rarely love life as it is either. Most people have come to prefer certain of life's experiences and deny and reject others, unaware of the value of the hidden things that may come wrapped in plain or even ugly paper. In avoiding all pain and seeking comfort at all cost, we may be left without intimacy or compassion; in rejecting change and risk we often cheat ourselves of the quest; in denying our suffering we may never know our strength or our greatness. Or even that the love we have been given can be trusted.

It is natural, even instinctive to prefer comfort to pain, the familiar to the unknown. But sometimes our instincts are not wise. Life usually offers us far more than our biases and preferences will allow us to have. Beyond comfort lie grace, mystery, and adventure. We may need to let go of our beliefs and ideas about life in order to have life.

The loss of an emotional or spiritual integrity may be at the source of our suffering. In a very paradoxical way, pain may point the way toward a greater wholeness and become a potent force in the healing of this suffering.

A woman with heart disease and chronic angina once told me of the downside of the surgery which had relieved her symptoms. Before this surgery, she had suffered frequent chest pain from her disease. Over the years she had modified her diet, learned to meditate, and had been successful in controlling most of her pain. Yet some of her pain had been resistant to her efforts. Paying very careful attention to this, she had been shocked to notice that she experienced pain when she was about to do or say something that lacked integrity, that really wasn't true to her values. These were usually small things like not telling her husband something that he did not seem to want to hear, or stretching her values a bit in order to go along with others. Times when she allowed who she really was to become invisible. Even more surprising, sometimes she would know this was happening but sometimes the chest pain would come first, and then, examining the circumstances which provoked it, she would realize for the first time that she had been betraying her integrity and know what it was that she really believed. She had learned a great deal about who she was in this way, and though she was physically more comfortable now, she missed her "inner adviser."

This is not actually so surprising. It is known that stress can affect us at the weakest link in our physical makeup. It raises the blood sugar in people who have diabetes, precipitates headaches in those with migraine, and stomach pain in people with ulcers. It causes people with asthma to wheeze and people with arthritis to ache. What is new in this story and so many others that I have heard is that stress may be as much a question of a compromise of values as it is a matter of external time pressure and fear of failure.

Unexplained pain may sometimes direct our attention to something unacknowledged, something we are afraid to know or feel. Then it holds us to our integrity, claiming the attention we withhold. The thing which calls our attention may be a repressed experience or some unexpressed and important part of who we are. Whatever we have denied may stop us and dam the creative flow of our lives. Avoiding pain, we may linger in the vicinity of our wounds, sometimes for many years, gathering the courage to experience them.

Without reclaiming that which we have denied, we cannot know our wholeness or have our healing. As St. Luke wrote in Acts of Apostles 4:11, the stone rejected by the builders may prove in time to be the cornerstone of the building.

What we believe about ourselves can hold us hostage. Over the years I have come to respect the power of people's beliefs. The thing that has amazed me is that a belief is more than just an idea—it seems to shift the way in which we actually experience ourselves and our lives. According to Talmudic teaching, "We do not see things as they are. We see them as we are." A belief is like a pair of sunglasses. When we wear a belief and look at life through it, it is difficult to convince ourselves that what we see is not what is real. With our sunglasses on, life looks green to us. Knowing what is real requires that we remember that we are wearing glasses, and take them off. One of the great moments in life is the moment we recognize we have them on in the first place. Freedom is very close to us then. It is a moment of great power. Sometimes because of our beliefs we may have never seen ourselves or life whole before. No matter. We can recognize life anyway. Our life force may not require us to strengthen it. We often just need to free it where it has gotten trapped in beliefs, attitudes, judgment, and shame.

HEALING AT A DISTANCE

People who are physicians have been trained to believe that it is a scientific objectivity that makes them most effective in their efforts to understand and resolve the pain others bring them, and a mental distance that protects them from becoming wounded by this difficult work. It is an extremely demanding training. Yet objectivity makes us far more vulnerable emotionally than compassion or a simple humanity. Objectivity separates us from the life around us and within us. We are wounded by that life just the same; it is only the healing which cannot reach us. Physicians pay a terrible personal price for their hard-won objectivity. Objectivity is not whole. In the objective stance no one can draw on their own human strengths, no one can cry, or accept comfort, or find meaning, or pray. No one who is untouched by it can really understand the life around them either.

Sir William Osler, one of the fathers of modern medicine, is widely quoted as having said that objectivity is the essential quality of the true physician. What he actually said is different and far more profound than that. The original quote was in Latin and it is the Latin word *aequanimatas* which is usually translated as "objectivity." But *aequanimatas* means "calmness of mind," or "inner peace." Inner peace is certainly the ultimate resource for those dealing with suffering on a daily basis. But this isn't something achieved by distancing yourself from the suffering around you. Inner peace is more a question of cultivating perspective, meaning, and wisdom even as life touches you with its pain. It is more a spiritual quality than a mental quality.

Years ago Joseph Campbell offered a workshop for physicians on the experience of the sacred. At one point in his presentation he showed us slide after slide of sacred images: paintings, statues, pottery, tapestries, and stained glass from many places and times. I remember one of these vividly. It was a particularly fine example of Shiva Nata Raja, a "Dancing Shiva" from the Lieden Museum in Zurich. Shiva is the Hindu name for the masculine aspect of God, and while these small bronze statues are common in India, few of us had seen this charming image before. Shiva, the god, dances in a ring of bronze flames. The hands of his many arms hold symbols of the abundance of spiritual life. As he dances, one of his feet is lifted high and the other is supported by the naked back of a little man crouched down in the dust, giving all his attention to a leaf he is holding between his hands.

Physicians are trained observers. Despite the great beauty of the dancing god, all of us had focused on the little man and the leaf and we asked Joseph Campbell about him. Campbell began to laugh. Still laughing, he told us that the little man is a person so caught up in the study of the material world that he doesn't even know that the living God is dancing on his back. There is a bit of that little man in all of us and certainly in most physicians. Thinking back on that scene, I wonder what was going through Campbell's mind.

Life is the ultimate teacher, but it is usually through experience and not scientific research that we discover its deepest lessons. A certain percentage of those who have survived near-death experiences speak of a common insight which afforded a glimpse of life's basic lesson plan. We are all here for a single purpose: to grow in wisdom and to learn to love better. We can do this through losing as well as through winning, by having and by not having, by succeeding or by failing. All we need to do is to show up openhearted for class.

So fulfilling life's purpose may depend more on how we play than what we are dealt. Jack Kornfield, the Buddhist teacher, describes a spiritual truth he learned at a bingo game he attended with his elderly parents in Florida. There on the wall, in huge letters, was a sign reminding the players, You Have to Be Present to Win.

MIRROR IMAGE

JESS IS A history professor who is one of identical twins, brothers whose strong physical resemblance often confuses their friends, even now at thirty-five. All through childhood they had been dressed alike and only their parents could tell them apart. When Jess's twin was diagnosed with malignant melanoma, Jess knew that he too would suffer this disease. It took two years for his cancer to show up, in almost the same place as Jamie's but on the opposite side. Mirror image. From the beginning, Jess believed that whatever happened to his brother would happen to him. One night a year after his own cancer diagnosis, I got a phone call from him. He told me that Jamie had found a lump in his groin. The cancer had spread. His voice shook slightly. "We will die," he said.

Indeed Jamie's struggle with cancer intensified, first chemotherapy, then after another recurrence, a bone marrow transplant, and after yet another recurrence, more chemotherapy. Through it all, Jess's anguish for his brother was augmented by the certainty that the other shoe must fall.

Since Jamie's diagnosis, Jess had worked to strengthen his sense of personal identity, but as his brother became sicker the older ways of thinking reemerged in all their power. He was not at all certain that he could survive Jamie's death. I had done everything possible to emphasize their differences. "We have bodies but we are not our bodies," I told him. He and his brother were each souls. They might share a common biology but they did not share a common destiny. This was intuitively clear to Jess but it did not change the bottom line. "The soul does not control the body," he told me. "We are biologically the same person and biology is destiny. It is only a matter of time."

The place in Jess which could not be moved was the place which held his earliest, most unconscious memories. After all, his brother had been with him since the beginning; the inviolateness which surrounds us all in the womb had surrounded them both. What were words or facts in the face of such profound joining? And yet what was the power of such a belief to influence the body? Was destiny mediated by biology or by belief? I did not know.

I began to hope for a sign, something that would speak in its own language to the deep place of belief in this highly sophisticated and intellectual man. Perhaps a dream? Or a portent?

In the end, it was simpler than that. In the midst of a session, Jess had been speaking of his experience of being a twin, the inability of others to know him from his brother, the constant struggle to be his own person. His brother had always tried to close the space between them. He himself had always tried to establish boundaries. He felt now that this had been futile. What hope was there for being your own person when chance had made you an identical twin? There could be no escape. In distress, he turned toward a shelf beside his chair on which I keep many small items given to me by my patients. Picking up the dice another client had left with me, he shook them hard and tossed them on the floor. "Chance!" he said bitterly.

The dice lay there on the rug, two perfectly identical cubes. One had come up a one and the other a six. We looked at them in silence. Then for the first time in months, Jess began to laugh. Sometimes all that is needed is a sense of possibility.

A GOOD FORTUNE

WHENEVER ANYTHING went wrong for the family my father would shake his head and say, "The luck of the Remens." He applied the phrase liberally and even-handedly to such things as losing a parking space as well as the larger things in life such as his bankruptcy and the chronic illness of his only daughter. The luck of the Remens was certainly not good luck. My father, who believed in nothing beyond a human agency in this world, felt life to be a random and dangerous enterprise and he felt overwhelmed by it. The luck of the Remens was invoked often. For many years I believed that we were unlucky people.

In 1971, my father won a prize in the New York State lottery. It was not a huge amount of money by lottery standards, but it was more money than my dad had ever seen in his life in one place. It was a windfall for him. It was a windfall for me, too, not because of the money but because of what happened next.

My father was in the hospital when he won the lottery, recovering from the removal of a tumor which turned out to be benign. He taped the winning ticket to his chest, saying that no one could be trusted to redeem it, not any of the family or any of his friends, not even my mother. He was convinced that someone would keep the ticket or it would be stolen from them or the people at the lottery office would not record it honestly once it was handed over. For a long time he could not be persuaded to turn the ticket in. As the deadline to redeem it got closer, he swore my mother and me to secrecy, telling us that people would try to take advantage of us in some way if they knew. Eventually he did redeem the ticket himself, but he never did spend the money because he was afraid that others would then know he had it.

Gradually, a very familiar anxiety settled around us. And then I got my windfall. I saw that the luck of the Remens was homemade. There was no way that my father *could* be lucky in this world. He could even turn winning fifty thousand dollars into a misfortune, a source of grief, anxiety, and stress. Until then, I had believed that we really were unlucky. Something gray that had hung over me all my life lifted. I have lived off my windfall from that lottery ticket ever since.

I had other windfalls from my father's life, other lessons about gain and loss. Actually, there is no one alive who has not had the experience of loss. We start learning about loss from the moment we are born. Often we take our family's attitudes toward it as I did. These lessons about loss and the meaning of loss are some of the most important things we will ever learn. This wisdom is rarely shared because when we lose we often feel ashamed.

My father was the son of immigrants. He had worked since childhood and held two jobs most of his adult life. In the evenings he would often fall asleep in his chair, his feet in a basin of warm water, too exhausted to talk. Always he had worked for other people, on their terms, for their goals. One of the earliest things I can remember is my father telling me how important it was to be your own boss, to be in control of your own life.

I grew up on the sixth floor of an apartment building in Manhattan. All through my childhood, there was a game my father and I would play. He would talk about his house, the house he would someday own. There would be a dishwasher in the kitchen. And a garden. We argued about whether the living room should be painted light green or be cream-colored. I favored cream. Dad thought it was too upscale.

I was almost twenty when he and Mom bought a little place on Long Island and he retired. For a while his dream seemed complete. Some months after the place was his, I stopped by on a Sunday visit and found him asleep exhausted in his chair. A familiar sight from my childhood, but I had thought that things would be different now. My mother told me he had just taken a little job, so that they could keep the place up. Things are always deteriorating.

On my next visit, he was asleep in his chair again. "Are you enjoying yourselves?" I asked. "Well," Mom said, "your father is afraid that someone will break in and take away everything we've worked for. He's still working because he wants to put in an alarm system." My heart sank. I asked how much it would cost. My mother evaded me and said they would have it in just a little while. Months later, my father continued to look weary. Concerned, I asked when they would be taking their vacation. My father shook his head. "Not this year—we can't leave the house empty." I suggested a house sitter. My father was horrified. "Oh no," he told me. "You know how people are. Even your friends never take care of your things the way they would take care of their own." They never took another vacation.

In the end, my parents rarely left the house together, not even to go to the movies. There could be a fire or some other sort of vague and unnamed disaster. And my father worked odd jobs until he died. The house turned out to have far greater control over him than any of his former employers ever had.

If we fear loss enough, in the end the things we possess will come to possess us.

GRACE

MY PATIENT, a physician who has cancer, comes to his session enormously pleased with himself. Knowing my love of stories, he says that he has found a perfect story and tells me the following parable:

> Shiva and Shakti, the Divine Couple in Hinduism, are in their heavenly abode watching over the earth. They are touched by the challenges of human life, the complexity of human reactions, and the ever-present place of suffering in the human experience. As they watch, Shakti spies a miserably poor man walking down a road. His clothes are shabby and his sandals are tied together with rope. Her heart is wrung with compassion. Touched by his goodness and his struggle, Shakti turns to her divine husband and begs him to give this man some gold. Shiva looks at the

man for a long moment. "My Dearest Wife," he says, "I cannot do that." Shakti is astounded. "Why, what do you mean, Husband? You are Lord of the Universe. Why can't you do this simple thing?"

"I cannot give this to him because he is not yet ready to receive it," Shiva replies. Shakti becomes angry. "Do you mean to say that you cannot drop a bag of gold in his path?"

"Surely I can," Shiva replies, "but that is quite another thing."

"Please, Husband," says Shakti.

And so Shiva drops a bag of gold in the man's path.

The man meanwhile walks along thinking to himself, "I wonder if I will find dinner tonight—or shall I go hungry again?" Turning a bend in the road, he sees something on the path in his way. "Aha," he says. "Look there, a large rock. How fortunate that I have seen it. I might have torn these poor sandals of mine even further." And carefully stepping over the bag of gold, he goes on his way.

It seems that Life drops many bags of gold in our path. Rarely do they look like what they are. I ask my patient if Life has ever dropped him a bag of gold that he has recognized and used to enrich his life. He smiles at me. "Cancer," he says simply. "I thought you'd guess."

SLEIGHT OF HAND

I REMEMBER a time when I was clearly playing the part of the little man studying a leaf who could not see that God was dancing on his back. In my final year of pediatric training, I had a twelve-year-old patient with aplastic anemia. One morning Carlos had awakened complaining of feeling tired. The next, he could not be awakened at all. When he was brought to our emergency room his hemoglobin level was 5, a third of what is normal. His marrow had suddenly and inexplicably stopped making red cells. At the time, such a condition was almost invariably fatal.

We hospitalized him immediately and began transfusing him. I was assigned this beautiful young boy during his hospitalization. Sick as he was, he was a delightful child, on the verge of manhood. He was an accomplished magician, amusing us and the children on his ward with his remarkable skills. He loved to fool his doctors; our baffled looks would make him giggle as he drew the ace of spades from our ears and made our quarters disappear. He was a master of illusion, and no matter how we tried we could not catch him at it. He charmed us all. His death was unthinkable.

A few months previously an experimental protocol for aplastic anemia had been developed which offered a slim hope of jump-starting the marrow. It required giving massive doses of testosterone. We used it. It made an enormous change in this beautiful child. He became hairy and coarse-featured, his face covered with acne and his voice deep and rough. His smile was gone and his magic with it. He was sullen and short-tempered. But life was at stake and so we continued.

After he left the hospital I followed him weekly in the clinics. No one else had wanted to do it. The senior residents had actually drawn straws; I had lost. Week after week, I could barely force myself to see him and confront the hope in his mother's eyes. Yet I carried him with me everywhere, haunted by his suffering and grieving for the boy who had so completely vanished. I read everything that was written about this mysterious disease, and everything that I read gave me the same bottom line: the prognosis was hopeless. In my heart I knew we could do nothing. Carlos would die.

The method of hemoglobin testing we used back then had a range of accuracy; whatever figure the lab gave us, the real number was plus or minus 0.2. A hemoglobin reported as 6 meant the patient's real hemoglobin lay somewhere between 5.8 and 6.2. It also meant that test results of 5.8, 6.0, and 6.2 could all reflect the same real hemoglobin. For this reason each lab slip reported the most recent test value and the results of the previous test for the purposes of comparison. Only an increase of more than 0.2 could be considered evidence that the bone marrow was responding and once again making blood. I explained all this to Carlos and his family.

The first clinic hemoglobin was 6, the same as it had been in the hospital. I met his mother's eyes and shook my head. The following week, 6 again. I shook my head again. And the next week, another 6. And then 6.2. Well within the error of the test method, I told them, and watched their hope drain away. It had been six weeks since the beginning of treatment. As each week went by it seemed more obvious to me that the medicine was not working and it was only a matter of time. The following week, Carlos's hemoglobin was 6.4. The lab slip reminded me that the previous week's value was 6.2. Once again I felt a pain in my heart as I shook my head. "Six point four," I told his mother, "well within the range of error of the test."

My certainty about Carlos's death and our failure to prevent it was so strong that I could only deal with it one week at a time. I wanted to run away. Week after week I would look at the new lab slip and refer back to the results of the week before. Each week the new results were well within the error of the testing method. Carlos's hemoglobin had risen to 7.4 before I recognized what was happening. And even then it was only because when I shook my head and gave his mother the bad news, she leaned forward and gently touched me on the arm. "Doctor," she said, "my boy is better, my boy is getting well!" And so he was. I was so certain he was dying that I had not been able to see. Our expectations may actually blind us. I have never been so certain of anything again.

THE EMPEROR'S NEW CLOTHES

A HUMAN LIFE has seasons much as the earth has seasons, each time with its own particular beauty and power. And gift. By focusing on springtime and summer, we have turned the natural process of life into a process of loss rather than a process of celebration and appreciation. Life is neither linear nor is it stagnant. It is movement from mystery to mystery. Just as a year includes autumn and winter, life includes death, not as an opposite but as an integral part of the way life is made.

The denial of death is the most common way we all edit life. Despite the power of technology to reveal to us the nature of this world, death remains the ultimate unknown, impervious to the prodding finger of science. We might well ask if anything which cannot be addressed in scientific terms is really worthy of our attention. Yet most of the things that give life its depth, meaning, and value are impervious to science.

In 1974 as I became interested in working with people facing death, I had thought to study death itself much as I had studied any other new field that had attracted my professional interest. I began in our library with a search of the current literature. The library serves a major medical school and hospital and is one of the largest and best medical libraries in the United States. Approaching a librarian, I asked if she could direct me to the periodicals on death. "Do you mean *Cancer Research* and the *Journal of Oncology*," she responded, "or the *American Journal of Cardiology*?" We stared at each other for a moment. "Death," I said.

Confused, she lowered her eyes and began to search her index under "D," finally coming up with a location deep in the library stacks. Following her instructions, I went downstairs past floors and floors of medical journals and books to the right floor. There, searching through rows of ceiling-to-floor shelves, filled with journals and periodicals, I found the section on death at last. It was a single shelf, almost empty, which contained five outdated issues of the *Journal of Thanatology*, two books on the pastoral counseling of the bereaved, and a copy of the New Testament.

After the initial shock, I remember thinking that I must be face-to-face with the Shadow of contemporary medicine. Surely the hundreds of thousands of journals and books I had just passed to get here might be thought of as a massive response to the possibility of death. Yet death itself was hidden, barely given shelf space in this vast body of knowledge which represented the state of the art of medicine. At that time, every library in every medical school in the United States was set up in this same way. Many still are.

At the time of my brush with death in the medical stacks, death occupied the same position in my consciousness that it occupied in the medical library. In fact, the medical library might have been an externalization of my own mind. As is true for most doctors, I had been present at a death only when my frantic efforts to prevent it had failed. I put these deaths behind me as quickly as I could and filled my mind with the countless facts about disease and cure on which my skills were based.

My first experience of death as something other than professional failure occurred when I was director of the pediatric inpatient division at Mount Zion Hospital, an inner-city hospital in San Francisco. I had not known then that death can be a time of healing, or that sometimes, shortly before people die, their wholeness can be directly experienced by others.

Arriving for work one morning, I was alarmed to hear angry voices coming through my closed office door. Inside, several of the staff nurses and resident doctors were arguing in an uncharacteristically emotional scene. The subject of this angry interchange was one of the patients, a five-year-old boy who was in the end stages of leukemia. Apparently this morning the child had told the nurse who awakened him that he was going home today. "Help me pack my things," he demanded, pointing with excitement to his tiny suitcase in the closet.

The nurse was horrified. Who could have promised this terribly sick little boy that he could go home when he had no platelets or white cells? When everyone knew he was so fragile he could bleed to death from the slightest injury? She asked the other nurses on her shift and the previous shift if they had told the child he might go home. No one had said a word to him.

The outraged nurses then accused the young doctors. The doctors were incensed at the suggestion that it was one of them who had callously promised such an impossible thing. The discussion had grown more heated then and was moved to the privacy of my office. "Could he go home by ambulance, just for an hour?" they asked me, unwilling to disappoint him and destroy his hopes. It seemed too dangerous. "Did anybody ask him who told him he could go home?" I said. Of course, no one had wanted to talk to him about that. I felt suddenly tired, but I said, "I'll go and talk to him."

He was sitting on his bed pillow, facing the door, and coloring in a book when I entered his room. I was struck by how emaciated, how sickly he was. He looked up from his coloring and our eyes met. In that moment things changed. The room became very still and there seemed to be a sort of yellowish cast to the light. I had a sense of an enormous presence and I remember thinking wildly that we had stepped outside of time. Suddenly I was aware of the overwhelming guilt I felt about this little boy. For months I had done things to him that caused him pain and I still had not been able to cure him. I had avoided him then and I felt ashamed. As our eyes met, it seemed that somehow he understood this and forgave me. All at once I was able to forgive myself, not just for this little boy but for all the children I had treated and hurt and couldn't help throughout my career. It was a sort of healing.

His frailty and my tiredness fell away and we seemed to recognize each other. In that moment we became equals, two souls who had played out our difficult roles in a drama with absolute impeccability; he as a little boy and I as a doctor. The drama was complete. It had served some unknown purpose and there was nothing to forgive or be forgiven. There was just a deep sense of acceptance and mutual respect. All this happened in a heart-beat.

Then he spoke to me. In a voice filled with joy, he said, "Dr. Remen, I'm going home." By now I was speechless. I mumbled something like, "I'm so glad," and I backed out, closing the door behind me.

I returned to my office very confused and shaken by the experience. "What did he say?" the staff demanded. I told them that I hadn't asked. "Why don't we just wait a little while and see what happens." A few hours later the child said he was tired. He lay down, pulling his sheet over his head, and quietly slipped away.

The staff took his death hard. He was a love of a little boy and they had cared for him for a long time. Yet many told me privately how relieved they were that he had died before he discovered that someone had lied to him and he couldn't go home.

Perception may require a certain openness. We see what our lives have made us ready to see. This child had known that he was going home in a much more profound sense than the staff was prepared to appreciate. At that time I had no way to make sense of this experience either, so I did the comfortable thing: I forgot it.

About a year after my trip to the library to study death I began to have a series of vivid, disturbing dreams. I would find myself once again at the bedside of pediatric patients who had died many years before. Before I went to sleep I would not have been able to remember these children's names, but in the dreams I would again know all of their lab values, be able to recall the pictures on their bedside tables, the names of their beloved stuffed animals, and even the pattern of their nightshirts. Unbidden, I would see clearly the many things that I had not fully seen when I had actually been there. I would hear again whole conversations, word for word, conversations filled with hope and fear, loss and love. I would see every nuance of expression on the faces of people whom I had not thought about in years. It was as if I had saved somewhere the experiences I had refused to live before. But the most frightening thing about these dreams was that eventually in each one I would come to feel what I had not allowed myself to feel, feelings of sadness, pain, helplessness, and loss. I would awaken sobbing uncontrollably, sometimes for hours.

These dreams occurred nightly. After four or five of them I called a friend who was a psychiatrist and poured out my concern and fright. I was afraid to go to sleep. Was I going crazy? "I don't think so," he said, and asked me if I felt willing to stay with it to see what it might mean. I was not sure that I could. "You can call me every morning and tell me about your dream," he offered. And so I did.

In the end I had twenty or more of these dreams. And gradually something changed. I began to know how much I had cared about these children, how meaningful and irreplaceable their lives had been, and to wonder if their deaths had any meaning also. Eventually I began to experience the great emptiness left by their passing and at last was able to genuinely wonder where they had gone. In the end I, who had taken death so personally, no longer saw it as personal failure but as universal mystery. I began to remember older experiences, experiences from my childhood, times before death was the enemy. I also remembered the little boy who had told me he was going home. Something inside me that had closed its eyes and run from death for years had turned again and wanted to see. To be there. As a preparation for my work with people who were facing life-threatening illness and possible death, these dreams turned out to be far more important than the expertise I had hoped to find in the library.

LAG TIME

THIRTY YEARS AGO, while I was still practicing medicine in New York City, I was taken to see a movie about Tibetan medicine. Tibet was hardly a household word back then and in the pressure of my training personal time was precious, but I went because I was in love with the man who invited me. I have never forgotten the film. It has taken me thirty years to begin to understand what it was about.

The film was a documentary, a day in a Tibetan clinic run by a young Tibetan doctor who was also a woman. Unlike my own clinic, on the first floor of a large concrete building, this clinic was high on a mountainside, reached only by an arduous and steep road. Prayer wheels stood every fifteen or twenty feet along this road, great cylinders covered with sacred words, which people struck in passing, sending them spinning and humming, wafting their blessings like perfume into the morning silence.

As I remember, the film begins at sunrise. The young physician is there in her clinic alone. She starts the day with prayers and then lights a flame in a huge bowl, signifying the opening of the clinic. We began our day at almost the same time with a quick cup of coffee, a sweet roll, and some light banter in the hospital cafeteria. As I watched, I felt a certain attitude begin to come over me, a sort of *National Geographic* consciousness. An unbridgeable distance started to open between me and the doctor I was watching in the movie.

Then the doors of the clinic were flung wide, and a great river of people flowed in, the old, the hurting, the very young, the dying, as well as the hopeful, anxious others who carried them and supported them. And I knew them. These were the same people I saw in my own clinic. This woman, in this foreign place with the most different of tools, was dealing with the same issues I dealt with every day. Perhaps these issues faced every doctor every day, everywhere. Fascinated, I watched her move through her work, listening, examining, diagnosing, treating, offering hope where there was hope and comfort where there was none. It was utterly and completely familiar and I could not understand a single word that was being said.

The film ends at the close of the clinic day, a time when I and my colleagues sat at our desks scrambling to catch up with our chart work. But the day ended very differently here. High in the mountains the sun is setting. The patients have gone; once again there is silence. The clinic helpers, young men, run swiftly down the road away from the clinic, striking the prayer wheels as they pass. One and then two more. And then a fourth, and a fifth. Then they are gone and the physician is once again alone. As darkness falls she chants a prayer in Tibetan, her words dropping one by one into the valley below. In the silence that follows she reaches out and extinguishes the flame in the great bowl.

In subtitles we were told that she was praying for the end of suffering, the *liberation of all sentient beings.* This baffled me. Was she praying for the death of all these people? How could someone so committed to healing end her day like this? And if she was not praying for death, then what was it she prayed for? Liberation made no sense to me at all. Now thirty years later it seems to me that there is a place where healing and freedom are one. I find that I, too, have come to hope for a medicine whose deepest commitment is liberation for us all, a medicine of human freedom.

IV.

Freedom

THE BUDDHISTS talk about samsara, the world of illusion. It is the place that most of us live. Mistaking illusion for reality is said to be the root cause of our suffering. Yet in some immensely elegant way suffering itself can release us from illusion. Often in times of crisis when we reach for what we have considered our strength we stumble on our wholeness and our real power. How we were before we fixed ourselves to win approval. What has been fixed is always less strong than what is whole. In a time of real need we may remember and free ourselves.

Integrity usually comes to people slowly and takes them unawares, as part of a natural process of maturing or through the need to be there for someone else who is counting on them. But it can appear full-blown in times of crisis or loss. In my work I have seen many people recover a greater integrity because they have lost something or someone very dear to them.

I remember walking down many a clinic corridor, an impatient, judgmental, and angry young person, and opening the door of an examining room. Waiting there would be an anxious mother and her sick child. Closing the door, I would become in that moment very much more the person I am now. Yet at thirty this was not my usual way of being. In the setting of my work, I was much more whole. As I knocked on that examining room door, I had access to a greater wisdom, compassion, and perspective than was mine only moments before. It was as if I could take a tuck in time. Such happenings are very common. They are often called forth by the needs of others.

With certain people we may get to try on a greater wholeness for a time, to actually experience being more. These experiences are a sort of grace. They help us to know not only the direction of our personal wholeness but how it feels and even tastes. Everyone's wholeness is unique and even such common role models as Eleanor Roosevelt and Albert Schweitzer can distance us from ourselves. Our wholeness will look different than theirs. Our wholeness fits us better than theirs. Our wholeness is much more attainable for us than theirs ever could be.

We usually look outside of ourselves for heroes and teachers. It has not occurred to most people that they may already be the role model they seek. The wholeness they are looking for may be trapped within themselves by beliefs, attitudes, and self-doubt. But our wholeness exists in us now. Trapped though it may be, it can be called upon for guidance, direction, and most fundamentally, comfort. It can be remembered. Eventually we may come to live by it.

We have all read stories about people stepping past lifelong limitations in response to extreme situations. Such an experience may happen to an entire nation at the same time. The stories that emerged out of England during World War II suggest that many English people had the experience of wholeness when under bombardment by the Germans. But most often the experience of wholeness happens in very ordinary times and ways. It is common to not even notice.

One of my patients, a young businessman with non-Hodgkin's lymphoma, was concerned from the moment of his diagnosis about how his wife would be able to manage both his illness and the possibility of his death. He described her as painfully shy and retiring, fragile even. They had eloped because she could not face having a public ceremony. He could not imagine how she would be able to deal alone with their children and with the very successful business he had developed.

When I first met her she was very much as he said. Yet as he struggled with the difficult chemotherapy, as he lost ground, as disappointment after disappointment led to his premature death, she underwent a remarkable change. It was she who supported him in taking risks, she who called doctors and other experts all over the country, who took over more and more of his business, learning as she went, who supported and comforted their children. Her courage, in both her personal and her business life, was as awesome as it was unexpected. By the time he died she was running the business, and afterwards continued to make a success of it alone.

A few years after he died, she called for an appointment. She wanted to discuss some decisions about her children's education and ask me if he had indicated any opinions that might serve as guidance for her now. The person who came to visit me was not the woman I had met only three years before. I commented on the changes and on the remarkable strength she had shown in dealing with her husband's illness and death and in making her own life. Had she known that she would be able to do the things she had done in the past few years?

"Well, no," she said, she had always been shy, and been labeled by others as shy from the time she was a small girl. So no one had ever challenged her and she had never challenged herself. Yet her courage and her ability to take risks had come very naturally to her. She had been surprised at first, but then she had decided that her courage was because of her shyness. She smiled.

"Rachel, I was so shy that it took courage for me to say hello to someone, it took courage to go to the supermarket and to the cleaners, it felt like a risk every time I answered the telephone. It took a lot of courage just to live, to do the things that other people do without thinking every day. I guess over the years my courage just grew from being used all the time like that. And when the time came that Jim needed me so badly, when I could no longer help him and be shy, why, I guess I was ready."

Some years ago a young resident psychiatrist from Langley Porter Institute at the UCSF Medical Center who wanted to learn more about people at the edge of life was observing one of my sessions. A former gang member whose hands were covered with tattoos was speaking of the deep love he now felt for his young wife who was dying of cancer, the ways in which this capacity to love had caught him unawares and so had healed him. As he shared insights about himself and experiences of intense intimacy and tenderness with his wife, I glanced over at the young Freudian psychiatrist. He had stopped taking notes. His eyes were filled with tears. After this patient left, I asked him if he had learned anything useful from the session. He smiled ruefully. "We are all more than we seem," he said.

Actually, we are all more than we know. Wholeness is never lost, it is only forgotten. Integrity rarely means that we need to add something to ourselves: it is more an undoing than a doing, a freeing ourselves from beliefs we have about who we are and ways we have been persuaded to "fix" ourselves to know who we genuinely are. Even after many years of seeing, thinking, and living one way, we are able to reach past all that to claim our integrity and live in a way we may never have expected to live.

Being with people at such times is like watching them pat their pockets, trying to remember where they have put their soul.

Two months after a diagnosis of breast cancer, a woman brought in a dream. She was standing before the eagle's cage at the Chicago Zoo watching a sleeping eagle on its perch. The cage, like all the other aviary cages, was made of something that looked like chicken wire but was much heavier and stronger.

As she watched, the eagle awoke. Spreading its magnificent wings, it flew through the wall of the cage. She watched it until it became a tiny spot against the sky. When finally it disappeared, she had no sense of loss but felt a lifting of her heart. It was then she noticed that there was no hole in the wall of the cage.

"A wonderful dream," I thought, and asked her what she made of it. She hesitated and then said that she was afraid of what the dream had meant. Did I think the dream meant that she was going to die? I said that I did not know but that it certainly was a dream about freedom. I suspected it might equally well mean that she was going to live.

Three years later this same woman, marveling over the inner changes and awakenings she had experienced since her diagnosis, told me, "Who would have thought I could have so much more joy in life and have cancer? Who would have thought that such a thing was possible?"

Often in reclaiming the freedom to be who we are, we remember some basic human quality, an unsuspected capacity for love or compassion or some other part of our common birthright as human beings. What we find is almost always a surprise but it is also familiar; like something we have put in the back of a drawer long ago, once we see it we know it as our own.

THE LONG WAY HOME

OFTEN TIMES of crisis are times of discovery, periods when we cannot maintain our old ways of doing things and enter into a steep learning curve. Sometimes it takes crisis to initiate growth.

I had as a patient a woman who was in her eighth year of recovery from cervical cancer. She had come weekly while she was undergoing cancer treatment but now we saw each other only for "touch-ups" when things became stressful for her. Helene was a truly gorgeous woman who spent hours on her appearance. Even during the worst of her chemotherapy and illness, her nails had been perfect, her wigs exquisite. No one had seen her face without makeup since she was a child. She had been single for several years. When she was married, she always awoke thirty minutes before her husband did to be fully made up and dressed before he opened his eyes.

The Holmes-Rahe Stress Index rates a promotion equal in stress to the loss of a job, and a marriage equal to a divorce. Perhaps it is change itself which stresses us whether it be loss or gain. Helene came to see me for one of her touch-ups because she had become engaged. She described her fiancé as a wonderful person—kind, loyal, intelligent, and humorous. He was a highly successful and creative businessman. They had been living together for some time and got on very well. She described him as "perfect" with one exception: he lacked passion. Their romantic life was "pleasant but boring." He asked her permission every time he kissed her. She was not sure that this was what she wanted in a man.

All this changed abruptly on October 17, 1989, at 5:04 P.M. On that afternoon, Helene was in one of downtown San Francisco's finest department stores seeking the perfect outfit for a business dinner honoring her fiancé. In the company of a personal shopper, she was in a dressing room wearing a fuchsia silk dress that she had decided was just right. Both women were admiring the dress, when the shopper suggested she wear it up to the seventh floor and match it to a pair of shoes. Leaving all her belongings in the locked dressing room, she went to the shoe department. She had just put on a pair of heels in the perfect shade when the earthquake struck.

All the lights went out. The building shook violently and she was thrown to the floor. In the darkness she could hear things falling all around her. When the shaking stopped, she, a few saleswomen, and several other customers somehow made their way down the stairs in the dark to the front door. There was broken glass everywhere.

Helene found herself standing in the street in a very expensive dress and perfectly matching four-inch heels. Frightened and dazed people rushed by her. All of her own clothes and her purse were somewhere in the dark chaos of a building which quite possibly was no longer safe to reenter. Her money was in her purse. So were her car keys. Walking to the corner, she picked up a public phone. It was dead.

Helene was a person who had never been able to ask for help, and she couldn't ask for help now. She turned north and started walking toward her home, many miles away in San Rafael.

It took her almost eight hours to reach there. After a short time her feet began to hurt, so she took off the heels and threw them away. As she walked on, her nylons tore and her feet began to bleed. She passed buildings that had collapsed, stumbled over rubble, waded through streets filled with filthy water from the fire-fighting efforts. Dirty, sweaty, and disheveled, she walked down the Marina to the Golden Gate Bridge and crossed it into the next county. She reached home sometime after midnight and knocked on her own front door. It was opened by her fiancé, who had never before seen her with her hair uncombed. Without a word he took her into his arms, kicked the door closed, covered her dirty, tearstained face with kisses, and made love to her right there on the floor.

Helene is a very intelligent person but she could not understand why she had never met this ardent lover before. When she asked him, he said simply, "I was always afraid of smearing your lipstick."

She tells me that now when she begins to relapse into her

former perfectionism, she remembers the look of love in her fiancé's eyes when he opened the door. She had been looked at by men all of her life but she had never seen that expression in a man's eyes before.

At the heart of any real intimacy is a certain vulnerability. It is hard to trust someone with your vulnerability unless you can see in them a matching vulnerability and know that you will not be judged. In some basic way it is our imperfections and even our pain that draws others close to us.

THE CONTAINER

OFTEN ANGER is a sign of engagement with life. People who are angry are touched deeply by the events of their lives and feel strongly about them. As an emotion, it has its limitations and it certainly has very bad press, but my experience with ill people suggests that there is something healthy about it. Certainly the cancer studies by Levy, Temoshak, and Greer suggest that many people who recover become angry first. Anger is just a demand for change, a passionate wish for things to be different. It can be a way to reestablish important boundaries and assert personal integrity in the face of a body- and life-altering disease. And, as it was for me, it may be the first expression of the will to live. Anger becomes a problem for people only when they become wedded to it as a way of life.

One of the angriest people I have ever worked with was a young man with osteogenic sarcoma of the right leg. He had been a high school and college athlete and until the time of his diagnosis his life had been good. Beautiful women, fast cars, personal recognition. Two weeks after his diagnosis, they had removed his right leg above the knee. This surgery, which saved his life, also ended his life. Playing ball was a thing of the past.

These days there are many sorts of self-destructive behaviors open to an angry young man like this. He refused to return to school. He began to drink heavily, to use drugs, to alienate his former admirers and friends, and to have one automobile accident after the other. After the second of these, his former coach called and referred him to me.

He was a powerfully built and handsome young man, profoundly self-oriented and isolated. At the beginning, he had the sort of rage that felt very familiar to me. Filled with a sense of injustice and self-pity, he hated all the well people. In our second meeting, hoping to encourage him to show his feelings about himself, I gave him a drawing pad and asked him to draw a picture of his body. He drew a crude sketch of a vase, just an outline. Running through the center of it he drew a deep crack. He went over and over the crack with a black crayon, gritting his teeth and ripping the paper. He had tears in his eyes. They were tears of rage. It seemed to me that the drawing was a powerful statement of his pain and the finality of his loss. It was clear that this broken vase could never hold water, could never function as a vase again. It hurt to watch. After he left, I folded the picture up and saved it. It seemed too important to throw away.

In time, his anger began to change in subtle ways. He began one session by handing me an item torn from our local newspaper. It was an article about a motorcycle accident in which a young man had lost his leg. His doctors were quoted at length. I finished reading and looked up. "Those idiots don't know the first thing about it," he said furiously. Over the next month he brought in more of these articles, some from the paper and some from magazines: a girl who had been severely burned in a house fire, a boy whose hand had been partly destroyed in the explosion of his chemistry set. His reactions were always the same, a harsh judgment of the well-meaning efforts of doctors and parents. His anger about these other young people began to occupy more and more of our session time. No one understood them, no one was there for them, no one really knew how to help them. He was still enraged, but it seemed to me that underneath this anger a concern for others was growing. Encouraged, I asked him if he wanted to do anything about it. Caught by surprise, at first he said no. But, just before he left he asked me if I thought he could meet some of these others who suffered injuries like his.

People came to our teaching hospital from all over the world, and the chances were good that there were some with the sorts of injuries that mattered to him. I said that I thought it was quite possible and I would look into it. It turned out to be easy. Within a few weeks, he had begun to visit young people on the surgical wards whose problems were similar to his own.

He came back from these visits full of stories, delighted to find that he could reach young people. He was often able to be of help when no one else could. After a while he felt able to speak to parents and families, helping them to better understand and to know what was needed. The surgeons, delighted with the results of these visits, referred more and more people to him.

Some of these doctors had seen him play ball and they began to spend a little time with him. As he got to know them, his respect for them grew. Gradually his anger faded and he developed a sort of ministry. I just watched and listened and appreciated.

My favorite of all his stories concerned a visit to a young woman who had a tragic family history: breast cancer had claimed the lives of her mother, her sister, and her cousin. Another sister was in chemotherapy. This last event had driven her into action. At twenty-one she took one of the only options open at that time, she had both her breasts removed surgically.

He visited her on a hot midsummer day, wearing shorts, his artificial leg in full view. Deeply depressed, she lay in bed with her eyes closed, refusing to look at him. He tried everything he knew to reach her, but without success. He said things to her that only another person with an altered body would dare to say. He made jokes. He even got angry. She did not respond. All the while a radio was softly playing rock music. Frustrated, he finally stood, and in a last effort to get her attention, he unstrapped the harness of his artificial leg and let it drop to the floor with a loud thump. Startled, she opened her eyes and saw him for the first time. Encouraged, he began to hop around the room snapping his fingers in time to the music and laughing out loud. After a moment she burst out laughing too. "Fella," she said, "if you can dance, maybe I can sing."

This young woman became his friend and began to visit people in the hospital with him. She was in school and she encouraged him to return to school to study psychology and dream of carrying his work further. Eventually she became his wife, a very different sort of person from the models and cheerleaders he had dated in the past. But long before this, we ended our sessions together. In our final meeting, we were reviewing the way he had come, the sticking points and the turning points. I opened his chart and found the picture of the broken vase that he had drawn two years before. Unfolding it, I asked him if he remembered the drawing he had made of his body. He took it in his hands and looked at it for some time. "You know," he said, "it's really not finished." Surprised, I extended my basket of crayons toward him. Taking a yellow crayon, he began to draw lines radiating from the crack in the vase to the very edges of the paper. Thick yellow lines. I watched, puzzled. He was smiling. Finally he put his finger on the crack, looked at me, and said softly, "This is where the light comes through."

Suffering is intimately connected to wholeness. The power in suffering to promote integrity is not only a Christian belief, it has been a part of almost every religious tradition. Yet twenty years of working with people with cancer in the setting of unimaginable loss and pain suggests that this may not be a teaching or a religious belief at all but rather some sort of natural law. That is, we might learn it not by divine revelation but simply through a careful and patient observation of the nature of the world. Suffering shapes the life force, sometimes into anger, sometimes into blame and self-pity. Eventually it may show us the freedom of loving and serving life.

ANOTHER KIND OF SILENCE

In the first year that I was a doctor, one of my patients was a fifteen-year-old girl with leukemia, who was the only child of older parents. At that time leukemia was not the treatable disease it is today. The available chemotherapy was very toxic and often a child had to be hospitalized for prolonged periods. This young girl had been hospitalized and treated many times, yet her disease continued to escape control. We were almost out of time.

Her chemotherapy was given intravenously, every four hours around the clock. Although it was ordered by her private doctor, we residents were the only doctors in the hospital twenty-four hours a day and so it fell to us to carry out the treatment. At a quarter to the hour, I went into the treatment room and prepared an IV of plain saline. Because her drug was extremely caustic in its undiluted form, I then put on a protective apron, protective goggles, a mask, and gloves. Outfitted rather like a knight in full armor, I would take the little bottle of cancer-killing drug from its locked storage place, open a fresh syringe, carefully draw up the exact amount needed, check this twice, and then inject it into the bottle of saline. Shedding the protective apron, mask, and goggles but still wearing the gloves, I would carry the diluted medication to Gloria's bedside, find a vein in her arm, and begin the infusion which slowly injected the poison directly into her bloodstream. I hated doing this.

My time with Gloria was made even more difficult because hospital policy back then was not to discuss the disease or the potential of death with a child without the parents' permission. Gloria's parents had emphatically not given their permission. They had posted a sign at the nurses' station reminding us not to discuss her disease or her prognosis. There was also a sign on the front of her chart. Their wishes were clear.

Barely twenty-four, I was only eight years older than my patient; we were two young women brought together by loss and the potential of death, but separated by a wall of silence as palpable as a thick sheet of glass. I could see Gloria, speak with her, and when I injected her chemotherapy, I could actually touch her, but each of us was terribly alone. During the night, Gloria's treatments fell at two A.M. and six A.M. and these times were especially difficult for me. Perhaps because of the darkness or the echo of my footsteps as I walked the sleeping ward, the loneliness seemed almost unbearable. I dreaded going in there.

The wall came down one night in a very natural way. Carrying Gloria's two A.M. dose, I went to her room, turned on the small lamp over her bed, and awakened her. She lay there in a pool of light, watching me as I set up for her IV. The needle went in easily; I taped it down and opened the stopcock. Gently I put her arm back under the blanket and asked her if she needed anything. Our eyes met. "Dr. Remen," she said, "am I dying?"

A great many things ran through my mind very quickly. I knew what I was supposed to say, but as I reached for the professional words of denial they just wouldn't come. Instead I told her that we were doing everything we knew, but the disease was still growing. If this continued, it was very possible that she might die. She closed her eyes for a moment and then she told me that she had known. She asked me not to tell her parents. She did not think they could bear it.

I asked her if she had thought much about dying. She nodded. "What is the hardest part about it for you?" She said it was not knowing what it was like to die. She asked if I had ever seen someone die. When I said that I had, she asked me to tell her about it.

At that time I had not seen many deaths, but I told her about the two deaths I had personally witnessed. She had not known that it did not hurt to die, and seemed very comforted. I asked her if it made her sad to talk like this and she said no, she had been sad a long time. She wanted to talk more. It was now almost morning. Promising that we would talk again when I returned at six with her next dose of medicine, I encouraged her to go to sleep now. Obediently, she closed her eyes. I left the light on.

At six, we began the first of a series of conversations about death. Her parents were not religious and what she had gathered from them when the dog had died was that death was the end. She missed the dog very much. Did I think death was the end? "Well," I said, "we don't really know," and presented death to her as I saw it, as mystery, telling her that it might be the end to life and then again it might not.

We wondered together: Could life go on in some other way? We spoke of heaven and other ideas about the possibility of life after death. She was surprised to learn that most of the people in the world believe that there is a life after death. I told her that philosophers and other people have always wondered about the mystery of death and written about it, and asked her if she would like me to bring her any of these writings. She accepted the offer.

For the next week or so we read and we talked. Sometimes one of her friends was there and we would all talk. Death was not a topic that had ever been discussed in my medical training. We had discussed the management of the dying patient, which is a different sort of thing. Yet I had been a philosophy major as an undergraduate. This choice had almost cost me admission to several top medical schools, but it was certainly coming in handy now.

I found myself looking forward to our meetings and listening to Gloria's thoughts and feelings. One evening she told me that she too looked forward to our talks and that she felt less afraid since we had begun to talk. I did not know a lot about psychology back then and it surprised me that simply talking together about something that had no resolution, no knowable answer, could have this effect. Although I had been well trained in diagnosing psychopathology, they had not taught me this about fear.

As the days passed it was obvious that the chemotherapy was

not controlling Gloria's disease. Her cell counts were rising and she felt weaker daily. I did not know her parents, as they communicated only with her private doctor and not with the house staff. As things began to go downhill I knew that I had to try to bring her together with them. I was a little anxious about this, as I had violated their express wishes by talking to her. This was simply not the way things should be done and I felt that they would justifiably be very angry. I had also violated hospital policy and not consulted with her private doctor or told him about our talks. If they complained to him, it might even mean my job. Still, it seemed only right to encourage her to speak with them now.

I asked Gloria how she would feel about talking to her parents and told her that I suspected they did not know she was thinking about her death. She asked if they knew she was dying and I told her that they did, but that they had not known how to talk to her about it. She said she felt she could talk to them now.

She reported to me that the first conversation had been very emotional. She was able to tell them that she felt she had let them down by becoming sick. They, good people that they were, told her how much she brought into their lives, and that they had no regrets. She had felt the depth of their love. She had always known how much her mother loved her but her father was undemonstrative; she had not known how deeply he cared. "Dr. Remen," she said, "he even cried."

Over the next few days they shared many private family memories. She told them things that had been important to her, things she had appreciated. Many of these things they had not even known. She had made a little will and she told them about it. She even spoke to them about her funeral and they planned it together. At her request, her father brought her a picture of the spot where she would be buried. He reminded her that someday he and her mother would be there too. It was terribly, terribly sad, but it was not lonely.

As the days went by and nothing was said to me, I began to relax. Although I had not asked her to keep our discussions secret, it seemed that Gloria had probably not told her parents about our talks. I felt a great relief.

Finally, Gloria slipped into a coma and died peacefully one morning just before dawn. Both her parents were with her. It was my night to cover the ward and so I had been awakened and was there when her private doctor arrived to sign the death certificate and talk to them. Conscious of his responsibility to train house staff, he invited me to join him in the counseling room and introduced me to Gloria's parents.

Both parents had obviously been crying. He assured them that everything possible, everything scientifically known had been done, but it just hadn't been enough. He told them sincerely how very sorry he was. He spoke of her courage and what good parents they had been to her. He spoke words of comfort. Both of them had been with her at the end, he said. She had not died alone. And she had not known she was dying, so she had not been afraid.

When he finished we all sat together for a while. Then her father looked at me for the first time.

"Thank you," he said.

She had not died alone, but it had been such a near thing.

GOING HOME

IN 1972, I was invited to be a subject in a research project conducted at the Esalen Institute by two educators, Sukie and Stuart Miller. At the time, the humanistic potential movement was at its height and Esalen was at the center of a paradigm shift that would ultimately influence the very foundations of our culture: education, politics, theology, the law, and of course medicine. It was host to such seminal thinkers as Gregory Bateson, Abraham Maslow, Aldous Huxley, Joseph Campbell, Alan Watts, Fritz Perls, and many others.

The research project was a twenty-four-month invitational fellowship offered to twelve established, conventional physicians. We were to have the opportunity to spend a weekend a month with one or another of these pioneering theorists, discussing new perspectives, experiencing new approaches, and attempting to see whether any of these new ideas about the nature and capacity of human beings had application to the practice of medicine.

At the time, I was a young professor, the associate director of the pediatric clinics at Stanford, and holistic health lay a dozen years in the future. I was certain of my professional direction. I was an academic pediatrician, one of the few women on the faculty at Stanford, and my ambition was to become the head of a department of pediatrics at a major medical school. I had joined the project not because I recognized it as the open doorway to my future but because at thirty-four it struck me as a rather good way to meet men.

It turned out to be one of the most important decisions of my life, a turning point toward almost everything of meaning that has followed. Despite a decade and a half of scientific training, long ago I had still been a philosophy major. Many of the unanswered questions of my college days, put away as secondary to the technology of my profession, reemerged with all their power and mystery at Esalen. I loved these weekends. Yet about six months into the fellowship I began to suffer panic attacks. After the third of these, a pattern became clear; they occurred a few days before I was to go to Esalen for the weekend. Shaken by these episodes, I went to Sukie Miller and attempted to resign.

But Sukie was wiser than this. A master therapist familiar with the ways in which people grow and the psychological phenomena that occur as the old way is lost and the new way not yet begun, she asked me if I was curious about why these things were happening. I was still sufficiently attached to my objectivity that I could not readily admit that all I wanted to do was run away. When I said that I would like to understand more, she offered to help me use imagery, a basic technique of the new psychologies we were exploring in the program, to uncover the meaning of these attacks.

We did a brief session. She asked me to close my eyes and encouraged me to allow an image to come to mind that related to my panic. Despite my skepticism about this new method, I found an image immediately: it was a thin, flat white rectangle. I described this to her, and with all the authority with which I was accustomed to making a rapid medical diagnosis, I added, "It's a business card." Sukie asked if I was sure. With horror I realized that I was not sure, that I didn't really know what this image was. With this realization came the beginnings of the dreaded panic feelings. I hastily opened my eyes. Sukie smiled at me in a comfortable way. She sympathized with my distress and told me that I could certainly resign from the project, but it might be best if I waited until the meaning of these episodes became clear. She suggested that I reflect on the thin white rectangle several times each day in my "downtime," wonder about it while waiting at stoplights or in line at the supermarket. She encouraged me to hold it in my mind and in a steady and undemanding way to be open to knowing what it meant. She assured me that its meaning would come to me in time.

It took four or five weeks, during which I was frustrated and irritable, convinced that this was all Sukie's clever manipulation to keep me in the research program and preserve the integrity of her data. But this was not the case. I can remember exactly where I was and what I was doing when the mystery resolved itself. I was driving up Gough Street, one of the steepest hills in

San Francisco, in a car with a standard transmission. All of my attention was focused on shifting gears without sliding backward into the car behind me. Suddenly, the flat white rectangle reappeared in my mind's eye, but this time it started to change shape, to puff up. This image was accompanied by all the chaotic feelings of a full-blown panic attack. Drenched in sweat, I pulled to the curb and parked. Terrified, I remember thinking, "I'm going to die here." And then I knew what it all meant.

The understanding came in the form of a story. The white rectangle was not a business card after all. It was a marshmallow that had been subjected to a steady external pressure for many, many years. The pressure had distorted its natural shape so that it was long and flat. But now, this pressure had been released. Its shape was changing and it was terrified. It felt as if it were dying. But the marshmallow was not dying, it was returning to itself. The shape that had been most familiar to it was not its own shape. With the lifting of the pressure, something deep in it could remember its integrity, its true shape, and was reclaiming it now. And somewhere there were other marshmallows that would now be able to recognize it and befriend it.

With this insight, the panic was gone and I knew a number of things with certainty. This childlike story had nothing to do with marshmallows, this was a story about me. My family had the highest regard for scholarship, academics, research, and teaching and a significant contempt for the nonrational. My medical colleagues felt the same. I had been under a lifelong pressure to conform to this way of being in the world. It was the price of belonging. I could do these things very well, and would always be able to do them but they were not my natural way, rather like writing with your right hand when you are a lefty. I had done them for so long and so successfully that I had not known that they were not my way, but I knew it with absolute certainty now.

The ideas of the Esalen program were transformational and the people I had met there were radically different from the people I had lived among for years. They were more like my grandfather and being with them had brought his presence back into my life. The integrity of their inquiry into the ineffable, their willingness to entertain questions that were larger than the available tools of research, had begun to release the pressure that had held me in a shape that was not my own. That shape was dying and I was changing back to a way of being that would fit me perfectly. Although I could be analytical and pragmatic, by nature I was an intuitive, even a mystic. I was my grandfather's granddaughter. I had remembered and I was going home.

The panic attacks never returned. Sukie did not seem surprised at all.

REMEMBERING

WHAT WE DO to survive is often different from what we may need to do in order to live. My work as a cancer therapist often means helping people to recognize this difference, to get off the treadmill of survival, and to refocus their lives. Of the many people who have confronted this issue, one of the most dramatic was an Asian woman of remarkable beauty and style. Through our work together I realized that some things which can never be fixed can still heal.

She was about to begin a year of chemotherapy for ovarian cancer, but this is not what she talked about in our first meeting. She began our work together by telling me she was a "bad" person, hard, uncaring, selfish, and unloving. She delivered this self-indictment with enormous poise and certainty. I watched the light play across her perfect skin and the polish of her long black hair and thought privately that I did not believe her. The people I had known who were truly selfish were rarely aware of it—they simply put themselves first without doubt or hesitation.

In a voice filled with shame, Ana began to tell me that she had no heart, and that her phenomenal success in business was a direct result of this ruthlessness. Most important, she felt that it was not possible for her to become well, as she had earned her cancer through her behavior. She questioned why she had come seeking help. There was a silence in which we took each other's measure. "Why not start from the beginning?" I said.

It took her more than eight months to tell her story. She had not been born here. She had come to this country at ten, as an orphan. She had been adopted by a good family, a family that knew little about her past. With their support she had built a life for herself.

In a voice I could barely hear, she began to speak of her experiences as a child in Vietnam during the war. She began with the death of her parents. She had been four years old the morning the Cong had come, small enough to hide in the wooden box that held the rice in the kitchen. The soldiers had not looked there after they had killed the others. When at last they had gone and she ventured from hiding she had seen that her family had been beheaded. That was the beginning. I was horrified.

She continued on. It had been a time of brutality, a world without mercy. She was alone. She had starved. She had been brutalized. Hesitantly at first, and then with growing openness, she told story after story. She had become one of a pack of homeless children. She had stolen, she had betrayed, she had hated, she had helped kill. She had seen things beyond human endurance, done things beyond imagination. Like a spore, she had become what was needed to survive.

As the weeks went by, there was little I could say. Over and over she would tell me that she was a bad person, "a person of darkness." I was filled with horror and pity, wishing to ease her anguish, to offer comfort. Yet she had done these things. I continued to listen.

Over and over a wall of silence and despair threatened to close us off from each other. Over and over I would beat it back, insisting that she tell me the worst. She would weep and say, "I do not know if I can," and hoping that I would be able to hear it, I would tell her that she must. And she would begin another story. I often found myself not knowing how to respond, unable to do anything but stand with her here, one foot in this peaceful calm office on the water, the other in a world beyond imagination. I had never been orphaned, never been hunted, never missed a meal except by choice, never violently attacked another person. But I could recognize the whisper of my darkness in hers and I stood in that place in myself to listen to her, to try to understand. I wanted to jump in, I wanted to soothe, I wanted to make sense, yet none of this was possible. Once, in despair myself, I remember thinking, "I am her first witness."

Over and over she would cry out, "I have such darkness in me." At such times it seemed to me that the cancer was actually helping her make sense of her life; offering the relief of a feared but long-awaited punishment.

At the close of one of her stories, I was overwhelmed by the fact that she had actually managed to live with such memories. I told her this and added, "I am in awe." We sat looking at each other. "It helps me that you say that. I feel less alone." I nodded and we sat in silence. I *was* in awe of this woman and her ability to survive. In all the years of working with people with cancer, I had never met anyone like her. I ached for her. Like an animal in a trap that gnaws off its own leg, she had survived—but only at a terrible cost.

Gradually she began to shorten the time frame of her stories, to talk of more recent events: her ruthless business practices, how she used others, always serving her own self-interest. She began to talk about her contempt, her anger, her unkindness, her distrust of people, and her competitiveness. It seemed to me that she was completely alone. "Nothing has really changed," I thought. Her whole life was still organized around her survival.

Once, at the close of a particularly painful session, I found myself reviewing my own day, noticing how much of the time I was focused on surviving and not on living. I wondered if I too had become caught in survival. How much had I put off living today in order to do or say what was expedient? To get what I thought I needed. Could survival become a habit? Was it possible to live so defensively that you never got to live at all?

"You have survived, Ana," I blurted out. "Surely you can stop now." She looked at me, puzzled. But I had nothing further to say.

One day, she walked in and said, "I have no more stories to tell."

"Is it a relief?" I asked her. To my surprise she answered, "No, it feels empty."

"Tell me." She looked away. "I am afraid I will not know how to survive now." Then she laughed. "But I could never forget," she said.

A few weeks after this she brought in a dream, one of the first she could remember. In the dream, she had been looking in a mirror, seeing herself reflected there to the waist. It seemed to her that she could see through her clothes, through her skin, through to the very depths of her being. She saw that she was filled with darkness and felt a familiar shame, as intense as that she had felt on the first day she had come to my office. Yet she could not look away. Then it seemed to her as if she were moving, as if she had passed through into the mirror, into her own image, and was moving deeper and deeper into her darkness. She went forward blindly for a long time. Then, just as she was certain that there was no end, no bottom, that surely this would go on and on, she seemed to see a tiny spot far ahead. As she moved closer to it, she was able to recognize what it was. It was a rose. A single, perfect rosebud on a long stem.

For the first time in eight months she began to cry softly, without pain. "It's very beautiful," she told me. "I can see it very clearly, the stem with its leaves and its thorns. It is just beginning to open. And its color is indescribable: the softest, most tender, most exquisite shade of pink."

I asked her what this dream meant to her and she began to sob. "It's mine," she said. "It is still there. All this time it is still there. It has waited for me to come back for it."

The rose is one of the oldest archetypical symbols for the heart. It appears in both the Christian and the Hindu traditions and in many fairy tales. It presented itself now to Ana even though she had never read these fairy tales or heard of these traditions. For most of her life, she had held her darkness close to her, had used it as her protection, had even defined herself through it. Now, finally, she had been able to remember. There was a part she had hidden even from herself. A part she had kept safe. A part that had not been touched.

Even more than our experiences, our beliefs become our prisons. But we carry our healing with us even into the darkest of our inner places. *A Course in Miracles* says, "When I have forgiven myself and remembered who I am, I will bless everyone and everything I see." The way to freedom often lies through the open heart.

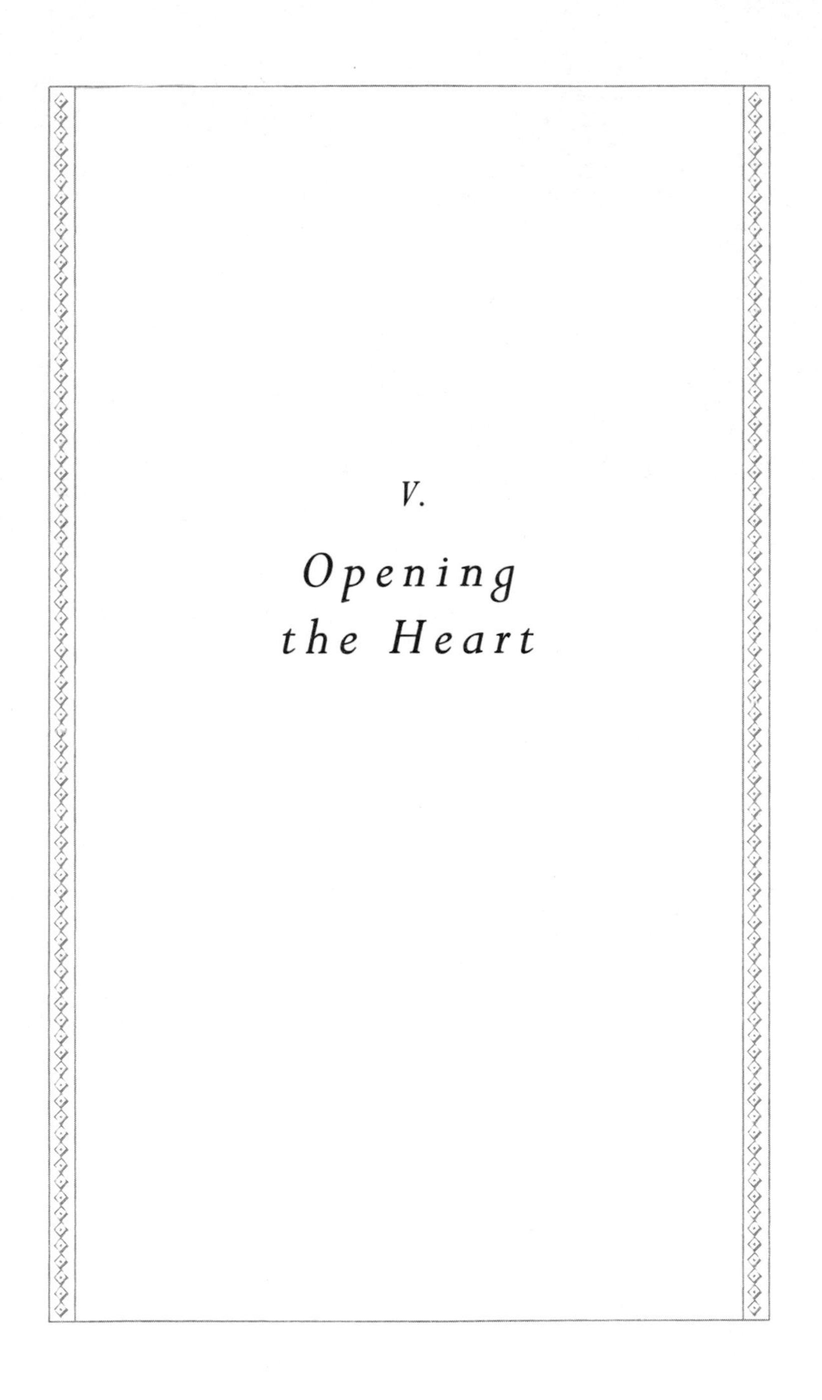

V.

Opening the Heart

MANY OF THE PEOPLE who come to talk about their cancer have ended up telling me that they have in some fundamental way felt alone all their lives.

They have felt loved and valued by others for what they can do but not for who they are, and they have loved and valued themselves in this same way. They have had relationships, lived among families, had neighbors, and worked with others, yet they have felt they have never really known the people around them or been known by them. Their cancer has made them aware of this for the first time.

Paradoxically, for some the profoundly isolating experiences of illness have begun to heal this sense of aloneness. Often this has come about slowly and not because of any deliberate action on their part, not by reading a book, taking a course, or even starting a meditative practice. Some people who have discovered the most genuine sense of connection, belonging, and altruism have discovered it completely by surprise.

One woman told me that she had found her way to the great simplicity of living with an open heart by crawling a long way on her knees in the dark. During her bone marrow transplant, she had felt a terrible anger, envy, and resentment, she had drowned in self-pity and experienced a vulnerability and sense of isolation so profound it had no words. She had never before allowed herself this depth of feeling, and she had felt overwhelmed by it. It had been frightening and painful, but in the end, it had burned away the habits of thought and belief that had separated her from other people, and left her with an unshakable sense of belonging and connection. In the midst of her suffering and helplessness she had one day simply known that all suffering was like her suffering and all joy was like her joy. From this has come an enduring inner change, a kindness that is almost involuntary.

Sharing many experiences of this sort with people has made me wonder about the nature of the heart. Perhaps the heart is not just a sort of valentine. More than a way of loving, the heart may be a way of experiencing life, the capacity to know a fundamental connection to others and see them whole. As with this woman, the opening of the heart seems to go far beyond love to an experience of belonging which heals our most profound wounds. When people look at others in this way, the connection they experience makes it a simpler thing to forgive, to have compassion, to serve, and to love. As my patient told me, "When I was able to connect honestly to myself, I found that I was connected to everyone else, too."

Perhaps the healing of the world rests on just this sort of shift in our way of seeing, a coming to know that in our suffering and our joy we are connected to one another with unbreakable and compelling human bonds. In that knowing, all of us become less vulnerable and alone. The heart, which can see these connections, may be far more powerful a source of healing than the mind.

A WAY OF LIFE

We are a nation of communicators, but communication is not always connection. I remember a scene in a Woody Allen movie where a group of lonely New York men sit around a table with beers, frantically talking to each other to ease their loneliness. Everyone talks at once. Gradually they raise their voices and interrupt each other trying to be heard. Finally they become so desperate that they are actually spitting on each other in their efforts to connect to each other, but they never do. This scene usually gets a laugh. I think more and more that life has become like this.

These days, disconnection is a habit, a way of life. I had not really felt how isolated I was until I spent a week in Fiji. Arriving at night and unpacking, I idly picked up the reading material left in my room by the hotel management. Under "Cultural Differences" I was surprised to find that it is considered good manners in Fiji to acknowledge total strangers on the street. The brochure was quite specific, telling me not to be alarmed if I found myself greeted by strangers, and indeed, people would think it rude if I did not respond in kind. The proper form was to make eye contact and acknowledge each other either by nodding and smiling or by saying, "Bu-la." In the place where I was raised, New York City, such a thing would be extremely unwise. Amused, I decided to try it.

What this means in practice is this: You walk down the street to the post office to buy a stamp for a postcard. On the way you might pass three or four people, greeting each one of them with a nod or a "Bu-la" and receiving their greeting. You buy your stamp, a transaction which takes only a moment. Walking back, you pass the *very same* people and it is expected that you greet them *again* even though you passed by only moments ago. Annoying at first, but by the end of a week it had become second nature.

Then I returned to the States. Rushing out to fill an empty refrigerator, I found myself on a busy street in California. All alone. No one made eye contact. No one greeted me. No one smiled. In some very profound way I felt both invisible and diminished. Yet the street was totally familiar. It was my home.

The Fijians are aware of a basic human law. We all influence one another. We are a part of each other's reality. There is no such thing as passing someone and not acknowledging your moment of connection, not letting others know their effect on you and seeing yours on them. For Fijians, connection is natural, just the way the world is made. Here, we pass each other with our lights out as ships in the night.

JUST LISTEN

I SUSPECT THAT the most basic and powerful way to connect to another person is to listen. Just listen. Perhaps the most important thing we ever give each other is our attention. And especially if it's given from the heart. When people are talking, there's no need to do anything but receive them. Just take them in. Listen to what they're saying. Care about it. Most times caring about it is even more important than understanding it. Most of us don't value ourselves or our love enough to know this. It has taken me a long time to believe in the power of simply saying, "I'm so sorry," when someone is in pain. And meaning it.

One of my patients told me that when she tried to tell her story people often interrupted to tell her that they once had something just like that happen to them. Subtly her pain became a story about themselves. Eventually she stopped talking to most people. It was just too lonely. We connect through listening.

When we interrupt what someone is saying to let them know that we understand, we move the focus of attention to ourselves. When we listen, they know we care. Many people with cancer talk about the relief of having someone just listen.

I have even learned to respond to someone crying by just listening. In the old days I used to reach for the tissues, until I realized that passing a person a tissue may be just another way to shut them down, to take them out of their experience of sadness and grief. Now I just listen. When they have cried all they need to cry, they find me there with them.

This simple thing has not been that easy to learn. It certainly went against everything I had been taught since I was very young. I thought people listened only because they were too timid to speak or did not know the answer. A loving silence often has far more power to heal and to connect than the most well intentioned words.

IN FLIGHT

AIRPORTS, even familiar airports, are very difficult to negotiate alone when you have lost a good deal of your eyesight as I have. Boarding a recent flight out of San Francisco, I sank into my seat with relief and belted myself in. I was seated at the bulkhead on the aisle. The window seat was occupied by an elegant older man. There was an empty seat between us. Looking to escape the tension of the past half hour, I put my purse on it, took out a murder mystery, and began to read. When lunch was served an hour later, I was deeply engrossed, the book inches from my nose. We were given a salad, a bagel, and a pint container of yogurt. Times have changed.

Continuing to read, I tucked into my plate until my seatmate gasped in dismay. Turning my head slightly, I saw that he had upset his full container of yogurt onto the floor, spilling it on his shoes, the rug, and part of his overnight bag. He was looking out of the window. I waited for him to take some action, but nothing happened. Looking down again, I saw that he was slowly drawing back his right foot, the shoe covered with yogurt, until it was almost hidden under the seat. I could now see his left foot clearly. His ankle was swollen and a metal brace emerged from his shoe. His left leg was paralyzed.

The seat belt sign was still on. I reached up and rang for the flight crew. No one responded. Some time later when the drink cart arrived, I indicated the floor and asked the stewardess for a wet towel. Before I could say anything more, she went ballistic: "There are four hundred and fifty-two people on this plane," she snapped. "I'm doing the best I can, you'll just have to wait." Her defensiveness baffled me. We looked at each other in silence. Then I realized that it had simply not occurred to her that I was a participant. "If you bring me a wet towel, I will be able to get that up," I said quietly. She hesitated and I wondered if she had heard. Then she raised her eyebrows, turned on her heel, and brought a towel. After the cart had passed us, I looked again at my seatmate. He continued to look fixedly out the window, his left foot motionless, his right hidden under the seat.

"I used to love to fly but I find it difficult now," I said, and I told him that in the past few years I have had trouble seeing. Still looking out the window, he told me that eight months ago he had suffered a stroke and now had no feeling in either of his arms from his fingertips to his elbows. Yet he had flown halfway across the country to spend some time in the home of his son. He was speaking almost in a whisper and I leaned toward him to hear. "Since my stroke I am incontinent," he said, "I have to wear a diaper." I nodded, marveling at the choreography of this chance seating arrangement. "I have an ileostomy," I said. He turned to look at me and asked what that was, and I explained that my large intestine had been surgically removed and I wear a plastic appliance attached to the side of my abdomen to collect my partly digested food. I added, "Even after thirty years, I am concerned that it may leak. Especially on a plane." After a moment, we smiled at each other. Then he looked at the towel I was holding and I looked down at his feet. As we talked he had brought his right foot out from under the seat. "May I?" I asked, motioning with the towel. Kneeling, I began to wipe his shoes. As I was doing this, he leaned forward and told me, "I used to play the violin . . ."

When I returned the towel to the galley, two flight attendants thanked me profusely. Later another, who was serving me a Coke, thanked me again. Nothing further was said but when I left the plane, the pilot was standing in the doorway. I smiled and nodded as always but he stopped me. "Thanks," he said, and pressed something into my hand. Halfway up the Jetway I looked at it. It was the little gift that the airlines often give to children after a flight, a pin in the shape of a pair of wings.

A flight crew deals with hundreds of thousands of Americans every year. Their surprised reaction to a simple act of kindness is chilling. Perhaps we are no longer a kind people. More and more, we seem to have become numb to the suffering of others and ashamed of our own suffering. Yet suffering is one of the universal conditions of being alive. We all suffer. We have become terribly vulnerable, not because we suffer but because we have separated ourselves from each other.

A patient once told me that he had tried to ignore his own suffering and the suffering of other people because he had wanted to be happy. Yet becoming numb to suffering will not make us happy. The part in us that feels suffering is the same as the part that feels joy.

TO BE SEEN BY THE HEART

WHEN WE ARE seen by the heart we are seen for who we are. We are valued in our uniqueness by those who are able to see us in this way and we become able to know and value ourselves. The first time I was seen this way I was very small, maybe three. I had never met my godfather. He lived in another city and when it was clear that he was dying I was taken to his home so that he could see me for the first time. My mother told me that I was going to meet my godfather and that he was dying. I was so small I didn't get the time sense quite right and understood that I was going to see someone who was dead. I looked forward to this for days.

I remember the details of this meeting very clearly, especially my godfather's bed. It was very high, higher than I could see, and made of a dark carved wood. My mother had lifted me up. Lying there among the pillows with his eyes closed was a very old man.

He was completely still and so thin that the covers didn't rise up over him very much. She put me down next to him, between him and the wall. She was talking to me softly but I wasn't listening. I watched him with interest. Then his daughter called to my mother from the kitchen and she turned away and went out into the hall for a short time to see what was wanted. In those few moments, my godfather opened his eyes and looked at me.

I remember how blue his eyes were, and how warm. In a voice that was barely more than a whisper he called me by my name. He seemed to be trying to say something more. I was very young then but I knew that whispers meant secrets, so I leaned toward him to hear. He smiled at me, a beautiful smile, and said, "I've been waiting for you."

My family were intellectual, formal, well-mannered people who were not openly affectionate or demonstrative. My godfather's eyes and his smile were full of a great love and appreciation. For the first time I felt a deep sense of being welcome, of mattering to someone. His hands were resting on the covers and, still smiling, he slid one a little toward me. Then he closed his eyes. After a short while he sighed deeply and was still again. I continued to sit there remembering his smile until my mother came back. She looked closely at my godfather and then snatched me up from the bed and ran with me from the room. My godfather had died.

My parents were deeply distressed about my being alone with my godfather when he died. It was the forties and they consulted a child psychologist to help me over the "trauma" of it. Yet my own experience had been quite different. It was many years before I could tell my parents what had really happened and how important it had been to me.

MAKING CARING VISIBLE

ONE OF THE MOST common things people with cancer tell me is that experiences of hospitalization and treatment are profoundly isolating. I suspect that this sense of aloneness may even undermine the will to live. When we feel the support of others, many of us can face the unknown with greater strength. I often use ritual to help people at times like this.

For more than twenty years I have offered a very simple yet powerful ritual to people before their radiation, chemotherapy, or surgery. I suggest they meet together with some of their closest friends and family the day before their procedure. It does not matter how large or small the group is, but it is important that it be made up of those who are connected to them through a bond of the heart.

Before this meeting I suggest they find an ordinary stone, a piece of the earth, big enough to fit in the palm of their hand,

and bring it to the meeting with them. The ritual begins by having everyone sit in a circle. In any order they wish to speak, each person tells the story of a time when they too faced a crisis. People may talk about the death of important persons, the loss of jobs or of relationships, or even about their own illnesses. The person who is speaking holds the stone the patient has brought. When they finish telling their story of survival, they take a moment to reflect on the personal quality that they feel helped them come through that difficult time. People will say such things as, "What brought me through was determination," "What brought me through was faith," "What brought me through was humor." When they have named the quality of their strength, they speak directly to the person preparing for surgery or treatment, saying, "I put determination into this stone for you," or, "I put faith into this stone for you."

Often what people say is surprising. Sometimes they tell of crises that occurred when they were young or in wartime that others, even family members, may not have known before, or they attribute their survival to qualities that are not ordinarily seen as strengths. It is usually a moving and intimate meeting and often all the people who participate say that they feel strengthened and inspired by it. After everyone has spoken the stone is given back to the patient, who takes it with them to the hospital, to keep nearby and hold in their hand when things get hard.

I have had several patients go to their chemotherapy, their radiation, or even their surgery with their stones strapped with adhesive tape to the palm of one of their hands or the bottom of their foot.

Over the years, many of the oncologists and surgeons in our

community have learned about these stones from their patients and are very careful about them. One surgeon even had the staff go through the hospital laundry in search of a stone that was accidentally thrown away with the sheets in the recovery room. I asked him why he had done this and he laughed and said, "Listen, I have seen people do badly after surgery and even die when there was no reason for it other than the fact that they believed they wouldn't make it. I need all the help I can get."

Actually, no one has chemotherapy or radiation or goes into an operating room without the thoughts, hopes, and prayers of many people going with them. The stone seems to make all that a little more plain to people and reminds them of the strength and beauty of what is natural. In an environment which is highly technical and sterile, it connects them to the earth. Ritual is one of the oldest ways to mobilize the power of community for healing. It makes the caring of the community visible, tangible, real.

NO STATUTE OF LIMITATIONS

YITZAK WAS A survivor. Liberated from a concentration camp in 1945, he had come to America, worked and studied hard, and was now a respected research physicist. His first words endeared him to me. His Slavic accent reminded me of some of the older people in my own family. Two years before, he had been diagnosed with cancer. Now he had come to our retreat for people with cancer to see if he could engage and possibly defeat this enemy with the power of his mind, the aspect of his being he trusted most profoundly.

At Commonweal we touch people a great deal more than was his custom. Disconcerted at first, he would ask, "Vat is all dis, all dis huggy-huggy? Vat is dis luff the strangers? Vat *is* dis?" But he let us hug him anyway. After a while he began to hug us back.

The Commonweal retreats last for a week. By the fourth day the inner silence which has been slowly generated by the daily yoga practice has become very deep, and spontaneous insights often arise. Sometimes this silence allows people to find their own truth for the first time.

On the fourth day, in the meditation which begins the morning session, Yitzak had an experience. It seemed to him that through his closed lids he could see a deep pinkish light, very beautiful and tender. Startled, he realized this light surrounded him and came in some mysterious fashion from his chest. When he told us about it later, he said it was like being inside of a big rose: very touching, because his last name means "little rose" in Polish.

In the moment, however, he became frightened. He was aware that the light had a direction, it was pouring out of his chest "like a big hemorrhage." It seemed to be coming from his heart and it made him feel vulnerable.

Yitzak had survived the concentration camps. For many years he had lived, as it were, in a world of strangers. A deeply loving person, since his experience as a boy, he had been very cautious with respect to his heart, loving only close people, only family. This way of living had helped him feel safer, had worked for him until now. But there is often fear behind such a wary lifestyle and now for the first time he had begun to feel some of this. It was uncomfortable for him.

The retreat staff dealt with his discomfort in the way they deal with everything else; they did not try to fix it, to explain away his experience or to interpret it for him. Instead they listened with interest and continued to support him as he tried to work out its meaning for himself. Over the next few days he seemed to relax more, to become more open.

Sunday, in the last session of the retreat, I try to tie up the loose ends. I knew Yitzak had been troubled by his experience, so I asked him how things were. He laughed. "Better," he said, and began to tell us of a walk he had taken on the beach the day before. In his mind, he had talked to God, asking God what all this was about, and had received comfort. Touched, I asked him what God had to say. He laughed again. "Ah, Rachel-le, I say to Him, 'God, is it okay to luff strangers?' And God says, 'Yitzak, vat is dis *strangers? You* make strangers. *I* don't make strangers.' "

There is no statute of limitations on healing. Forty years ago because of his life experiences Yitzak had closed his heart, the same way Ana had as an orphan in Vietnam. Now as he sought a way to heal his body, he had begun to heal in other ways as well. In the struggle to survive our wounds, we may adapt a strategy of living which gets us through. Life-threatening illness may cause us to reexamine the very premises on which we have based our lives, perhaps freeing ourselves to live more fully for the first time.

THE TASK GETS BETWEEN US

THE WAYS WE LOSE each other can be very simple. One of my patients describes how he spent time with his son prior to his cancer. "We would hike a mountain, a difficult climb, side by side, both focused on reaching the top. Then we would come down a different way, one behind the other to the car, and drive home. We did this many times. In thinking back, I have a clear memory of many of these climbs, but no memory of anything my son said to me or I to him."

In child psychology what this man is describing is called parallel play and is normal for children between two and three. At this age, children use the same sandbox and even the same toys, but they are playing alone, next to each other and not with each other. Rather than relate to each other, they relate to a common activity which they do in parallel.

My patient makes a great contrast between this and the way he and his son relate now. "I can't do much just now, so we sit and talk. I ask him about his life and how he feels about it. For the first time I know what is important to him, what sort of a man he is, what keeps him going. And I talk to him too. I know now that I am important to him, that he wants to spend time with me and not because we can do physical things together. Sometimes we just sit together, being alive. The mountain got between us before. I had not known that."

Many people live their lives in this way, sharing homes, jobs, and even families with others, but not connecting. It is possible to be lonely in the midst of a family, in your own home. Too often we even practice medicine this way. Side by side, patient and physician focus on the disease, the symptoms, the treatments, never seeing or knowing each other. The problem gets in the way and we are each alone.

SURPRISED BY MEANING

HARRY, an emergency physician, tells this story. One evening on his shift in a busy emergency room, a woman was brought in about to give birth. The nurses rapidly wheeled her into a room and paged him immediately. He had been in the room next door. As he entered, they rushed out past him to call her obstetrician. One look and Harry realized that their call was probably too late. If her obstetrician wasn't already somewhere in the building, Harry was going to get to deliver this baby himself. He likes delivering babies, and he was pleased. The nurses had returned and were hastily opening the delivery packs. The woman's husband had also arrived and the nurses seated him by his wife's head. They stood on either side of Harry, supporting her legs. The baby was born almost immediately.

While the little girl was still attached to her mother, Harry laid her along his left forearm. Holding the back of her head in his left hand, he took a suction bulb in his right and began to clear her mouth and nose of mucus. Suddenly, the baby opened her eyes and looked directly at him. In that moment, Harry stepped past his technical role and realized a very simple thing: that he was the first human being this baby girl had ever seen. He felt his heart go out to her in welcome from all people everywhere and tears came to his eyes.

Harry has delivered hundreds of babies. He has always enjoyed the challenges of delivery, the excitement of making rapid decisions and feeling his own competency, but he says that he had never let himself experience the meaning of what he was doing before. He feels that in a certain sense this was the first baby that he had ever delivered. He says that in the past he would have been so preoccupied with the technical aspects of the delivery, assessing and responding to needs and dangers, that he doubts he would have noticed the baby open her eyes or have registered what her look meant. He would have been there as a physician, but not as a human being. It was possible, now, to be both. He wonders how many other such moments of connection he has missed. He suspects there may have been many.

The power of a personal sense of meaning to change the experience of work, of relationship, or even of life cannot be overestimated. Viktor Frankl, in his ground-breaking book on the concentration camps, *The Search for Meaning,* reports that survival itself may depend on seeking and finding meaning. In the camps, those who were able to maintain a sense of meaning and purpose in their suffering were more able to survive the deprivation and atrocities of their daily lives than others for whom their suffering was meaningless.

Meaning may become a very practical matter for those of us who do difficult work or lead difficult lives. Meaning is strength. Physicians often seek their strength in competence. Indeed, competence and expertise are two of the most respected qualities in the medical subculture, as well as in our society. But important as they are, they are not sufficient to fully sustain us.

A great Italian psychiatrist, Roberto Assagioli, wrote a parable about interviewing three stonecutters building a cathedral in the fourteenth century. The effect of their sense of personal meaning on their experience of their work is the same as the effect meaning has for us today. When he asks the first stonecutter what he is doing, the man replies with bitterness that he is cutting stones into blocks, a foot by a foot by three quarters of a foot. With frustration, he describes a life in which he has done this over and over, and will continue to do it until he dies. The second stonecutter is also cutting stones into blocks, a foot by a foot by three quarters of a foot, but he replies in a somewhat different way. With warmth, he tells the interviewer that he is earning a living for his beloved family; through this work his children have clothes and food to grow strong, he and his wife have a home which they have filled with love. But it is the third man whose response gives us pause. In a joyous voice, he tells us of the privilege of participating in the building of this great cathedral, so strong that it will stand as a holy lighthouse for a thousand years.

The important thing in this parable is that all three of the expert stonecutters are doing the same repetitive physical task. Cutting stones. In the same way, Harry had delivered baby after baby. Competence may bring us satisfaction. Finding meaning in a familiar task often allows us to go beyond this and find in the most routine of tasks a deep sense of joy and even gratitude.

LINEAGE

We have not only lost one another, we have become isolated from the past as well.

I spent one afternoon talking to a Tibetan friend about the gratitude the Buddhist practitioner feels toward his teachers, his awareness of the living chain of service through which the wisdom has been passed since the Buddha lived twenty-five hundred years ago. I was touched by his experience of the continuity of his lineage, his intuitive sense of the presence of those who have passed the light of the teachings to him. I was especially struck by something he said toward the close of the conversation. "Rachel, our lineage is our strength."

It is not something that I have thought much about as a physician. There is such great pride in the power we have at present, the hard-won technological tools of diagnosis and treatment, that the past tends to be seen as primitive and outmoded.

A sort of computer age mentality of almost instant obsolescence.

The following day I was teaching at the medical school, an interconnected group of massive white buildings set on the top of a hill. In the midst of an intense discussion of the future of medicine, the anxieties accompanying the advent of managed care, the fears of time pressure and financial considerations eroding the excellence of care, the paranoia of government control and big-business intervention, I found my thoughts once again returning to the idea of lineage and I began to present this idea to the medical students. I told them about my Tibetan friend, his experience of the destruction of Tibet by the Chinese Communists and his belief in the importance of lineage in times of chaos and crisis.

I reminded them that our medical center, with its commitment to teaching, research, and service, stands in a direct and unbroken lineage to the temples of Aesculapius, the father of medicine. This first medical center also stood on a hill and people came from throughout the known world to study, to uncover the hidden secrets of healing, and to be healed. No writings from this period survive and the earliest known description of the temples is found in the writings of Cicero, who notes that in the central courtyard of the temples there stood a statue of Venus, the goddess of love. I remind them that for all its technological power, medicine is not a technological enterprise. The practice of medicine is a special kind of love. I tell them that our lineage can become our strength. And our healing.

SOME THINGS ARE OURS FOREVER

More than ten years ago, an eighty-five-year-old widower came to see me to discuss his feelings about whether or not to have surgery for a cancer confined to one lobe of his lung. After an agonizing period in which he examined his options, he decided that despite the risks he would have this operation. At peace with his decision, he asked me if I thought there was anything he could do to promote his healing after the surgery.

We spoke of exercise and diet and the possibility of Chinese herbs and acupuncture. Curious, I asked him how he had found the strength to go ahead with this difficult decision. He told me of a daydream that he had had a few weeks earlier. He had been sitting in his chair in the evening, reading his paper, and had almost nodded off. It seemed to him that his wife had come to sit with him. She looked much as she had in the early days of their long relationship, and as she looked at him he was struck by the love he could see in her eyes. As they sat together he could feel his fear easing a little and then he noticed that one of his oldest friends had also come into the room and was standing behind his wife's chair. His face too reflected the love that had cemented their lifelong friendship. He was smiling at this friend when he saw his brother standing beside him, his eyes filled with love too.

One by one, others whose lives had touched his in a loving way were there, family and friends, teachers and students, children and grandchildren, and even the family pets. It had been a long life and in the end there were more than fifty or sixty of them, crowding into the living room and even into the hall. In this way he had known that his life had been of value to many others and found that it was of value still. No longer alone with his decision, he felt fear release him and knew then that the surgery was the right thing for him to do, no matter if he survived it or not.

I could feel tears in my eyes. Looking at this lovely old gentleman, I could easily see that his life had meant a great deal to those who shared it. "What a beautiful thing," I told him. "Yes," he said, "and most of those people are dead now." He smiled at my look of surprise. "I guess anything good you've ever been given is yours forever." He nodded his head and then sat quietly, smiling to himself.

All lives touch many others. Sometimes this network is very large, sometimes small, but somewhere in it a certain quality of love is needed if we are to be able to survive. It is not a question of numbers. Sometimes it can be given by only one person. I often ask patients where the love that has sustained them has come from. For one man, the child of an abusive and alcoholic family, it was his dog.

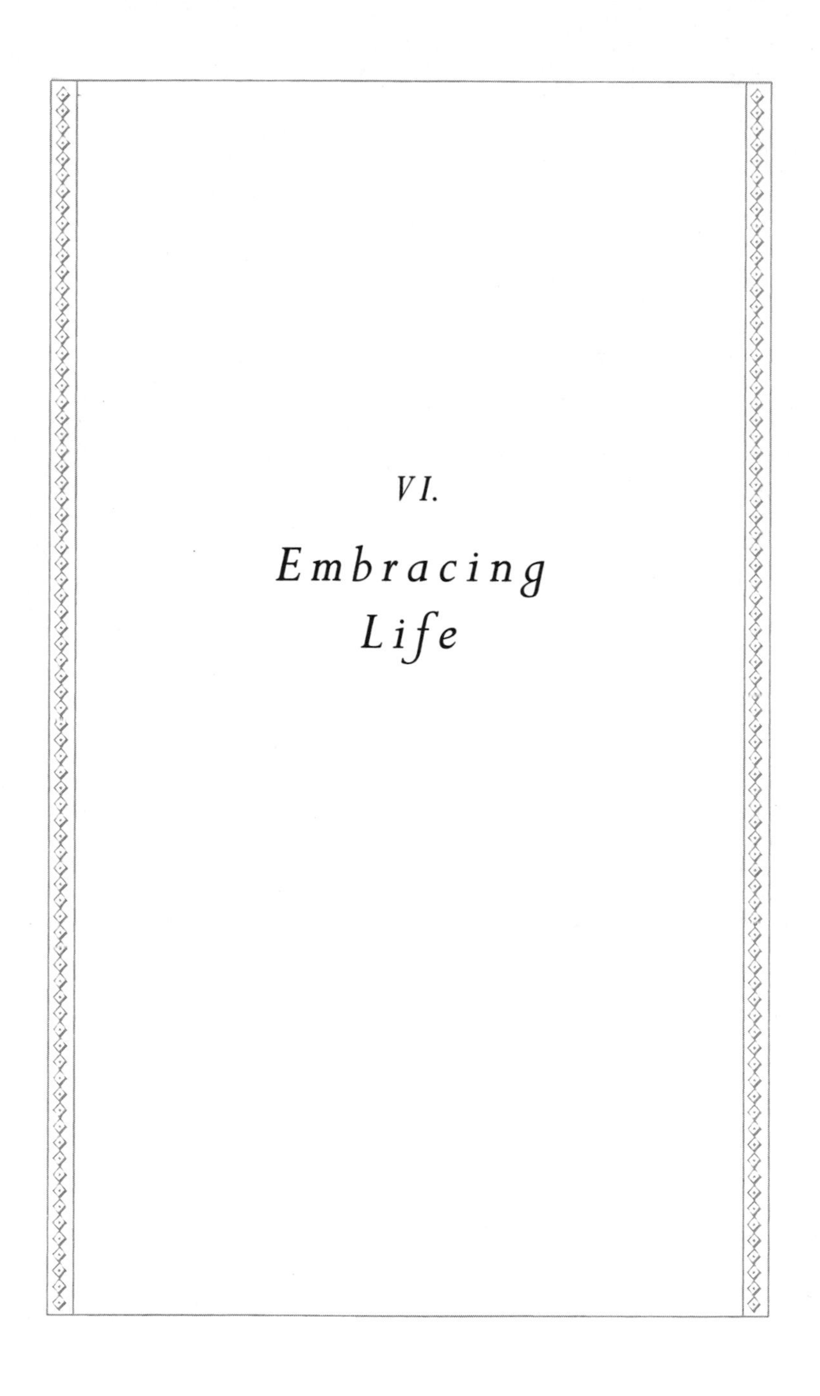

VI.

Embracing Life

All through my childhood, my parents kept a giant jigsaw puzzle set up on a puzzle table in the living room. My father, who had started all this, always hid the box top. The idea was to put the pieces together without knowing the picture ahead of time. Different members of the family and visiting friends would work on it, sometimes for only a few minutes at a time, until after several weeks hundreds and hundreds of pieces would each find their place.

Over the years, we finished dozens of these puzzles. In the end I got quite good at it and took a certain satisfaction in being the first one to see where a piece went or how two groups of pieces fit together. I especially loved the time when the first hint of pattern would emerge and I could see what had been there, hidden, all along.

The puzzle table was my father's birthday present to my mother. I can see him setting it up and gleefully pouring the pieces of that first puzzle from the box onto the tabletop. I was three or four and I did not understand my mother's delight. They hadn't explained this game to me, doubtless thinking I was too young to participate. But I wanted to participate, even then.

Alone in the living room early one morning, I climbed on a chair and spread out the hundreds of loose pieces lying on the table. The pieces were fairly small; some were brightly colored and some dark and shadowy. The dark ones seemed like spiders or bugs, ugly and a little frightening. They made me feel uncomfortable. Gathering up a few of these, I climbed down and hid them under one of the sofa cushions. For several weeks, whenever I was alone in the living room, I would climb up on the chair, take a few more dark pieces, and add them to the cache under the cushion.

So this first puzzle took the family a very long time to finish. Frustrated, my mother finally counted the pieces and realized that more than a hundred were missing. She asked me if I had seen them. I told her then what I had done with the pieces I didn't like and she rescued them and completed the puzzle. I remember watching her do this. As piece after dark piece was put in place and the picture emerged, I was astounded. I had not known there would be a picture. It was quite beautiful, a peaceful scene of a deserted beach. Without the pieces I had hidden, the game had made no sense.

Perhaps winning requires that we love the game unconditionally. Life provides all the pieces. When I accepted certain parts of life and denied and ignored the rest, I could only see my life a piece at a time—the happiness of a success or a time of celebration, or the ugliness and pain of a loss or a failure I was trying hard to put behind me out of sight. But like the dark pieces of the puzzle, these sadder events, painful as they are, have proven themselves a part of something larger. What brief glimpses I have had of something hidden seem to require accepting as a gift every last piece.

We are always putting the pieces together without knowing the picture ahead of time. I have been with many people in times of profound loss and grief when an unsuspected meaning begins to emerge from the fragments of their lives. Over time, this meaning has proven itself to be durable and trustworthy, even transformative. It is a kind of strength that never comes to those who deny their pain.

. . .

Over the years I have seen the power of taking an unconditional relationship to life. I am surprised to have found a sort of willingness to show up for whatever life may offer and meet with it rather than wishing to edit and change the inevitable. Many of my patients also seem to have found their way to this viewpoint on life.

When people begin to take such an attitude they seem to become intensely alive, intensely present. Their losses and suffering have not caused them to reject life, have not cast them into a place of resentment, victimization, or bitterness. As a friend with HIV/AIDS puts it, "I have let go of my preferences and am living with an intense awareness of the miracle of the moment." Or in the words of another patient, "When you are walking on thin ice, you might as well dance."

From such people I have learned a new definition of the word "joy." I had thought joy to be rather synonymous with happiness, but it seems now to be far less vulnerable than happiness. Joy seems to be a part of an unconditional wish to live, not holding back because life may not meet our preferences and expectations. Joy seems to be a function of the willingness to accept the whole, and to show up to meet with whatever is there. It has a kind of invincibility that attachment to any particular outcome would deny us. Rather than the warrior who fights toward a specific outcome and therefore is haunted by the specter of failure and disappointment, it is the lover drunk with the opportunity to love despite the possibility of loss, the player for whom playing has become more important than winning or losing.

The willingness to win or lose moves us out of an adversarial relationship to life and into a powerful kind of openness. From such a position, we can make a greater commitment to life. Not only pleasant life, or comfortable life, or our idea of life, but all life. Joy seems more closely related to aliveness than to happiness.

The strength that I notice developing in many of my patients and in myself after all these years could almost be called a form of curiosity. What one of my colleagues calls fearlessness. At one level, of course, I fear outcome as much as anyone. But more and more I am able to move in and out of that and to experience a place beyond preference for outcome, a life beyond life and death. It is a place of freedom, even anticipation. Decisions made from this perspective are life-affirming and not fear-driven. It is a grace.

To the degree that we can relinquish personal preference, we free ourselves from win/lose thinking and the fear that feeds on it. It is that freedom which helps a team to go to the Super Bowl. An adversarial position may not be the strongest position in life. Freedom may be a stronger position than control. It is certainly a stronger and far wiser position than fear.

There is a fundamental paradox here. The less we are attached to life, the more alive we can become. The less we have preferences about life, the more deeply we can experience and participate in life. This is not to say that I don't prefer raisin toast to blueberry muffins. It is to say that I don't prefer raisin toast so much that I am unwilling to get out of bed unless I can have raisin toast, or that the absence of raisin toast ruins the whole day. Embracing life may be more about tasting than it is about either raisin toast or blueberry muffins. More about trusting one's ability to take joy in the newness of the day and what it may bring. More about adventure than having your own way.

AT LAST

Two days before my mother's eightieth birthday I asked her how she wanted to spend the day. "I want to climb to the top of the Statue of Liberty," she replied. "Isn't there an elevator?" My mother looked at me. "I want to climb the stairs," she said.

She had lived in New York City for almost eighty years but she had never had this experience. She clearly remembered her first view of the "Liberty" when she had sailed into the New York harbor from Russia. She had been five years old then. Now, of course, she had a severe heart condition, and there were 342 steps to the top. Undaunted, I realized we could do it three or four steps at a time, resting in between. We would take her nitroglycerin and simply allow all day. When I proposed this to Mom she was delighted.

During the six-hour ascent, I had many misgivings. How had I gotten into this crazy thing, climbing the Statue of Liberty with an eighty-year-old woman with severe heart disease? But it was her wish and so we continued, a few steps at a time. She may have had angina but she also had an iron will. I think half of New York must have passed us on those stairs.

Finally, unbelievably, we were six or seven steps from the top. As we stood there taking what must have been our three-hundredth time-out, my mother eyed the last few steps between her and her goal with resentment. "Why," she said, "couldn't we have done these first?"

In thinking of this story now, I remember all the times that I too have resented the climb, the amount of living needed to gain the precious understanding to know how to live well. And how important it is in the struggle for freedom from the old ways not to be limited by style or self-expectations or to worry about what others may think. To be willing to do the really important things any way you can, even three steps at a time.

I NEVER PROMISED YOU A ROSE GARDEN

My BACKYARD ON the slopes of Mount Tamalpais in Northern California is actually a very small meadow. In the summer and fall of every year a stag visits at dawn and at twilight. This is quite a thing for someone who grew up in Manhattan. This year he has six points on his antlers. Last year five or perhaps four. He is heart-stopping.

Actually, I did not plan to have a stag, I planned to have a rose garden. The year after I moved here, I planted fifteen rosebushes, gifts from my friends. It was a lot of hard work, but I could see it in my mind's eye. Just like in *Sunset* magazine. The roses bloomed in the late spring and for a month the garden was glorious. Then the roses started disappearing. Puzzled, I eventually realized that something larger than aphids was eating them and became determined to catch it in the act. Getting up one dawn and glancing out the window, I was transfixed by seeing the stag for the first time. He looked like an illustration from one of my childhood books. As I watched in awe he unhurriedly crossed the yard, browsed for a while among the roses, and then delicately ate one of my Queen Elizabeths.

Every year since then I have had to make a difficult choice. Am I going to put up higher fences and have roses, or am I going to have a stag ten feet from my back door? Every year so far, I have chosen the stag. After two years of watching each other through a pane of glass, I can now sit outside as he dines.

If I tell people this, some say in disbelief, "You mean that you are letting this deer eat your roses?" Sometimes I will invite someone like this over to watch. One friend, stunned into silence by the sight, said simply, "Well, I guess we are always doing the right things for the wrong reasons." I had thought I was planting rosebushes in order to have roses. It now seems I was actually planting rosebushes in order to have half an hour of silence with this magical animal every morning and every evening.

One of my patients, a woman with ovarian cancer, told me this: "Before I got sick, I was very certain of everything. I knew what I wanted and when I wanted it. Most of the time I knew what I had to do to get it too. I walked around with my hand outstretched saying, 'I want an apple.' Many times life would give me a pomegranate instead. I was always so disappointed that I never looked at it to see what it was. Actually, I don't think I could have seen what it was. I had the world divided up into just two categories: 'apple' and 'not-apple.' If it wasn't an apple, it was only a not-apple. I had 'apple eyes.' "

Embracing life is actually a choice. When asked to describe

her husband, another of my patients, laughing, tells this story about a visit to Hawaii that has become part of her family's mythology. An organized and frugal man, her husband had reserved compact rental cars on each of the four islands months in advance. On arriving on the Big Island and presenting their reservation to the car rental desk, they were told that the economy car they had reserved was not available. Alarmed, she watched her husband's face redden as he prepared to do battle. The clerk did not seem to notice. "I am so sorry, sir," he said. "Will you accept a substitute for the same price? We have a Mustang convertible." Barely mollified, her husband put their bags in this beautiful white sports car and they drove off.

The same thing happened throughout their holiday. They would turn in their car and fly to the next island, only to be told that the car they had been promised was not available and offered a same-price substitution. It was amazing, she said. After the Mustang, they had been given a Mazda MR-10, a Lincoln Town Car, and finally, a Mercedes, all with the most sincere apologies. The vacation was absolutely wonderful and on the plane back, she turned to her husband, thanking him for all he had done to arrange such a memorable time. "Yes," he said, pleased, "it was really nice. Too bad they never had the right car for us." He was absolutely serious.

LIFE IS FOR THE WELL

One of my patients who has Chronic Fatigue Syndrome spent several years seeking help for her symptoms, going from doctor to doctor obsessed with the minutest details of her physical problems, which she tracked in a daily journal. She no longer does this. What she had thought was that you had to be without symptoms to enjoy life, to go to the theater, to have children, to love. It was as if life was only lived by well people, could only be lived by well people. In meditation, it came to her that her chronic disease was not stopping her from participating in life, but the meaning she had assigned to it, that she could not participate in life because of it, was far more limiting than the disease itself. She was surprised to realize that there was absolutely no reason why if she felt weak or was in some pain, she couldn't still go to the theater. It might take her longer to get to her seat.

Once there, if she felt too poorly, she might have to leave early. She might even have to miss the last act. One never knew. But the meaning she had assigned to her symptoms was causing her to miss the whole play.

She has stopped pursuing the perfect health she once had and does what she can to strengthen her body in simple, natural ways. Instead of seeing four or five doctors a week, she now consults her doctors only for serious problems. She has discovered that by being willing to begin without being certain of the outcome, she is often able to do a great deal more than she would have thought. Laughingly, she says that she has made a substitution in the cross-stitched sampler that hangs on the walls of her inner life. It used to say, "Life is only for the well." Now it says, "Anything worth doing is worth doing half-assed."

A ROOM WITH A VIEW

AFTER COMPLETING the last treatment in a year of potent chemotherapy one of my clients went to San Francisco overnight with her husband to celebrate. Her oncologist had tried to discourage her from this. It had seemed rather pointless to him, as she was still far too weak to see the sights, go to a restaurant, or participate in any of the fabled activities of this rich and complex city. He couldn't imagine why she might want to go if she could not do these things, and he had suggested she wait a few months until she was stronger. But she and her husband had gone anyway and stayed in a nice hotel.

Afterwards, I asked her about it. "It was wonderful," she said. "First we ordered room service. They brought it in on a table with a cloth a half-inch thick. My first meal without a tray. It was so elegant, the wineglasses and the butter carved into little flowers. And the food! We sat in this lovely room overlooking a little park and ate real food that I could actually taste. In the nude. Then we made love. Then we took long, long hot baths and used up every single towel in the bathroom. Great big thick towels—there were twelve of them. And we used up all those delicious-smelling things in the little bottles. And watched both movies. And ate most of what was in the little refrigerator. And sat outside on the terrace in our bathrobes and saw the moon rise over the city. We found all the pillows that they hide in the dresser drawers and slept in this king-size bed with eight pillows. And saw the sunrise. We used it all up. It was glorious!" she said to me, a woman who spends most of the time in a hotel room asleep.

THREE FABLES ON LETTING GO

I.

FOR MANY YEARS I tried to persuade my father to buy a new living room couch. Year after year, the old green couch grew shabbier and shabbier. Finally it was no longer safe to sit on. Embarrassed, I told Dad that I had ordered a new couch from Macy's by phone. I was sending a photograph of it for their approval. If they liked it, it would be delivered on Friday. They loved it. Saturday I called. How did it look? Shamefacedly, my father told me he had canceled the order. It turned out that he didn't know what to do with the old couch. I suggested calling Macy's and telling them to take it away. He told me that they did not do that in New York.

"Then how about the Salvation Army?" Apparently they only took away the things they could still sell. Who would want our couch? With a sinking heart, I suggested looking in the yellow pages for someone who does hauling. But Dad didn't want a stranger to know how to get into his house.

Finally I was silenced. My father, unaccustomed to letting go of anything, could not find his way to accepting my gift. Several years later, in the night, the old couch collapsed in on itself. It stood in the living room that way until my father died and I brought my mother to live with me in California.

II.

The house I own is a little A-frame cabin in the foothills of a mountain outside of San Francisco. When I bought it, it was so cramped and shabby that the first friend I brought to see it blurted out, "Oh Rachel, you bought *this?"* I started throwing things away the day after I moved in, and for the next few years I threw away all sorts of things: light fixtures, toilets, staircases, doors. Eventually, I even took out some ceilings and a few of the walls.

The house had belonged to a man who was proud of his ability to fix things. If there was a hole in the wall, he picked up the first available board and nailed it there. If his wife wanted a shelf or a door or a deck, he put one wherever she pointed. I threw all these things away.

Oddly, the more I threw away, the more I seemed to have. Over time, I rented four large grange boxes and filled them with everything that did not belong. As I let go of each of these things, I could imagine my father saying, "Just a minute, that still works, you never know when you'll need one of those." Gradually, the house became simpler, more empty, and the beautiful structural lines of its basic form began to emerge. It became a container for the light. In the end, all that was left was the wholeness. I painted it white.

III.

Jane's dog was never more than two feet away from her. Gentle, brown, and devoted, it even slept on her bed at night. Its devotion was returned full measure, and when it died of old age, my friend said that she doubted she would ever have another dog. She didn't have another dog for several years.

During this time I visited her often in the small town where she lived. Sunday afternoon we would walk down to the beach together. In those few blocks, she would stop to pat dogs on leashes, and strays would come up joyfully to greet her. Each got a moment of tenderness and a dog biscuit from her pocket.

Once I asked her if she missed her dog. "Yes," she said, "very much." But then she told me something odd. When she had a dog there were two kinds of dogs: her dog and all the other dogs. Now it seems as if all dogs are her dog.

ENDBEGINNINGS

I WAS THIRTY-FIVE years old before I understood that there is no ending without a beginning. That beginnings and endings are always right up against each other. Nothing ever ends without something else beginning or begins without something else ending. Perhaps this would be easier to remember if we had a word for it. Something like "endbegin," or "beginend."

For a long time I never noticed the beginnings. That was one of the first things that changed for me when I entered the Institute for the Study of Humanistic Medicine, the Millers' research program at Esalen. At that time, I was just learning how to make jewelry and had cast a silver ring. The design was the head of a woman whose long hair, entangled with stars, wound around your finger and formed the ring shank. Technically, it had been difficult to make and I was proud of the design. I finished it in time to wear to one of the first weekend sessions at Esalen.

The ring attracted a great deal of admiration and attention. At that time many craftsmen were in residence at Esalen, and several suggested that I drive back up the coast a few miles and show it to the jeweler at a gallery we had passed next to the road.

It was about to rain, but I made the trip anyway and had a wonderful afternoon. The jeweler, a gentle man and a gifted artist, had offered me tea and we spent an hour or so talking about beauty and the ways in which art reminds people of the soul. Heady conversation for a young academic physician. In the end, I left my ring with him so that he could recast it and sell it to others. I drove back down Route 1 with difficulty. Some serious rain had begun and the wind was strong enough to push my car a little on the road.

During the night, a wild and violent storm, the last of a long series of winter storms, hit the coast. At breakfast, without electricity and heat, I was shocked to hear that we were isolated. A stretch of Route 1 north of Esalen had fallen into the ocean. We would have to drive many miles south and go inland in order to go north to get back to San Francisco.

The gallery where I had left my ring had stood next to the stretch of road that had washed into the Pacific. The building was gone and my ring with it.

Through my numbness, I could hear several inner voices commenting on my loss. The loudest was my father's saying, "This never would have happened if you hadn't allowed a total stranger to exploit you and make a profit from your design. How stupid can you be, and you a doctor?" And my mother: "You are so careless! You can never be trusted with anything valuable. You always forget things and lose things." Mixed in was the voice of a very young part of myself that kept looking at the place on my hand where the ring had been yesterday and saying, "Where *is* it? It was right *here.*"

In anguish, I went to the edge of the cliffs and stood looking at the Pacific, still wild from yesterday's storm. Down there somewhere was my ring. As I watched the ocean hammer the cliffs, it began to occur to me that there was something rather natural, even inevitable, about what had happened. Pieces of the land had been falling into the ocean for millions of years. Perhaps all those familiar blaming voices were wrong. There was nothing at all personal in it, just some larger process at work.

I looked at the place on my finger again. This time it really was an empty space. And silent. It was big. For the first time I faced a loss with a sense of curiosity.

What would come to fill up this space? Would I make another ring? Or would I find another ring in a secondhand shop, or even in another country? Perhaps someday someone I had not even met would give me a ring because he loved me.

I was thirty-five years old and I had never trusted life before. I had never allowed any empty spaces. Like my family, I had believed that empty spaces remained empty. Life had been about hanging on to what you had and medical training had only reinforced the avoidance of loss at all costs. Anything I had ever let go of had claw marks on it. Yet this empty space had become different. It held all the excitement and anticipation of a wrapped Christmas present.

SURRENDER

JOAN'S HYSTERECTOMY for cervical cancer was her fifth surgery. Shortly after her thirty-fifth birthday, she had entered into a battle with time, a plastic surgeon at her side. With his skill she had stripped back the years, reclaiming the eyes, the chin, and even the breasts and bottom of her youth. Unwilling to grow old, she examined her face and body constantly, exercised daily, and was on a continual diet. We were the same age but she looked fifteen years younger. "No one really needs to grow old," she had told me. "Aging is a choice."

The battle for her life began with a positive Pap smear. The cancer had been diagnosed early and a year of strenuous chemotherapy and radiation had put it into remission. It had been a tough year. Six months after she completed her cancer treatment, we finished our own work together. At the time, her hair was just beginning to grow back.

Several years afterwards, in the local market, I was stopped by a handsome gray-haired woman I did not recognize. She greeted me warmly. Seeing my puzzled look, she burst out laughing. "It's Joan," she told me, still chuckling. "I'm growing old. Who would think that someone like me could be so grateful to have wrinkles."

ATTACHED OR COMMITTED

THIRTY-FIVE YEARS AGO, I had as a patient a young man who had become separated from his ski party and spent three days in below-zero weather yet somehow had managed to survive. He had been hospitalized for several days in the ski country, and then flown to our center in New York because of frostbite and progressive gangrene of his feet. The local surgeons had wanted to amputate and it was hoped that our world-renowned vascular surgical team could avoid this difficult choice. He had some initial surgery and for three weeks the outcome was not clear. Then his left foot began to improve and his right became steadily worse. The time for amputation at hand, the young man flatly refused. He preferred to keep his foot.

Gradually he became sicker and sicker as the toxins from his injured foot began to flood his body. His family and friends were desperate, but he would not be moved. He would keep his foot. The situation came to a head late one evening when for the third or fourth time a group of doctors shared his most recent laboratory studies and reviewed his worsening condition with him. In the midst of this discussion his fiancée, overwhelmed by the possibility of her beloved's death, was driven beyond her endurance. Weeping, she tore his engagement ring off her finger and thrust it onto the swollen black little toe of his right foot. "I hate this damned foot," she sobbed. "If you want this foot so much why don't you marry it? You're going to have to choose, you can't have us both." We all looked at the small bright diamond, surrounded by the black and rotting tissues of his foot. Even under the fluorescent lights, it sparkled with life. The young man said nothing and closed his eyes with weariness. Weary ourselves, we left to continue the medical rounds. The next day, he scheduled his surgery.

I continued to follow him through the fitting of his artificial foot and his rehabilitation. At the end of a year, only a slight limp marked his difficult choice. Two weeks before his wedding I revisited that final medical conference with him, asking him what had changed his mind. He said that seeing the diamond on his toe had shocked him. Jenny had been right. He had been married to his foot. Her dramatic gesture had helped him to see for the first time that he was more attached to keeping his foot than he was committed to his life, to their life together. Yet it had been the promise of that life that he had clung to, that had enabled him to survive three days alone in the snow.

While attachment has its source in the personality, in what the Buddhists refer to as the "desire nature," commitment comes from the soul. In relationship to life, just as in human relationships, attachment closes down options, commitment opens them up. Modern life has made us people of attachment rather than people of commitment. Indeed, many people have found that it is difficult to tell the difference between attachment and commitment in their own lives. Yet attachment leads farther and farther into entrapment. Commitment, though it may sometimes feel constricting, will ultimately lead to greater degrees of freedom. Both involve in the moment an experience of holding, sometimes against the flow of events or against temptation. One can distinguish between the two in most situations by noticing over time whether one has moved through this activity or this relationship closer to freedom or closer to bondage. Attachment is a reflex, an automatic response which often may not reflect our deepest good. Commitment is a conscious choice, to align ourselves with our most genuine values and our sense of purpose. Survival in a setting of life-threatening illness may involve a willingness to let go of everything but life itself.

EATING THE COOKIE

ANOTHER OF MY PATIENTS, a successful businessman, tells me that before his cancer he would become depressed unless things went a certain way. Happiness was "having the cookie." If you had the cookie, things were good. If you didn't have the cookie, life wasn't worth a damn. Unfortunately, the cookie kept changing. Some of the time it was money, sometimes power, sometimes sex. At other times, it was the new car, the biggest contract, the most prestigious address. A year and a half after his diagnosis of prostate cancer he sits shaking his head ruefully. "It's like I stopped learning how to live after I was a kid. When I give my son a cookie, he is happy. If I take the cookie away or it breaks, he is unhappy. But he is two and a half and I am forty-three. It's taken me this long to understand that the cookie will never make me happy for long. The minute you have the cookie it starts to crumble or you start to worry about it crumbling or about someone trying to take it away from you. You know, you have to give up a lot of things to take care of the cookie, to keep it from crumbling and be sure that no one takes it away from you. You may not even get a chance to eat it because you are so busy just trying not to lose it. Having the cookie is not what life is about."

My patient laughs and says cancer has changed him. For the first time he is happy. No matter if his business is doing well or not, no matter if he wins or he loses at golf. "Two years ago, cancer asked me, 'Okay, what is important? What is really important?' Well, life is important. Life. Life any way you can have it. Life with the cookie, life without the cookie. Happiness does not have anything to do with the cookie, it has to do with being alive. Before, who made the time?" He pauses thoughtfully. "Damn, I guess life *is* the cookie."

CHOOSE LIFE!

See, I have set before you this day the choice; good and evil, the blessing and the curse, life and death. Therefore, choose Life!

—Deuteronomy

Sometimes we may need to simply choose life. It is possible to become so attached to something or someone we have lost that we move forward blindly, looking over our shoulder to the past rather than before us to what lies ahead. The Bible tells us that as she looked back, Lot's wife was turned into a pillar of salt. I suspect that many of us have had this happen to us without our realizing we have become frozen, trapped by the past. We are holding to something long gone and, hands full, are unable to take hold of our opportunities or what life is offering.

Seven months after that first morning when he awoke with a dry cough, Dan died of pancreatic cancer, leaving behind a large group of stunned and grieving friends. His lover, in whose house he ultimately died, was devastated. She sat in his room for hours, and wore only the clothes that belonged to him. She withdrew from others. She went to his grave daily and lay on it, full-length on the ground.

While these are ways of grieving that are old and quite traditional, as the months slipped by and this behavior continued her family became concerned. I first saw her almost a year after Dan died. At that time her pain was as fresh as it was the morning after his death.

I listened but she had very little to say. She was hardly functioning, barely caring for herself. Although she went to work every day, she could not think clearly or initiate anything new. She described her work situation as precarious and felt that she would soon be terminated. She didn't seem to be able to care about this.

Her numbness was contagious. Sitting with her, I too felt a sense of heaviness and inertia, a lifelessness which made it hard to initiate a question or even to think. Before she came to see me she had been treated by one of the most competent psychiatrists in our community. He diagnosed her as having reactive depression, and treated her with a series of progressively more powerful antidepressive medications. Nothing had helped.

In some way her own life had stopped when her beloved had died. I began to talk to her about this stopping, asking her to describe how she felt inside. Over time she offered me several images of her inner experience. Once she told me that she had "circled the wagons, and they are still circling." Another time she told me that she felt she had swallowed her own energy, and when I gave her paper and crayons asking her to draw this, she drew a picture of a snake which had swallowed its tail.

The evening after this session I found myself thinking of this image again and again. I felt somehow that it was a Rosetta stone, the key to her whole situation, but I did not know how this might be. Furthermore, the image seemed familiar to me but I could not remember where I had seen it before. Puzzled, I went to one of Joseph Campbell's books and found that this was the Uroboros, a symbol associated with first chakra energy, the energy of survival. I began to wonder if in a time of loss we may instinctively reinvest our energy back into ourselves until we are certain that we can survive our wounds. Could we possibly become so totally focused on sustaining ourselves that we lose the impulse to move forward and connect to the world around us? Perhaps this was the situation of this young woman. Her apparent lifelessness and inertia might not reflect a lack of energy but simply be a sign that all her life force was circling back into herself, out of fear that she might not survive her great loss.

If so, no one had been able to break into this closed system and reengage her with her life, not even her former psychiatrist with all of the power of contemporary psychotropic medications. Perhaps such a system could open only from the inside; and she might be able to break out where no one had been able to break in.

At her next visit I began to talk to her about survival. Did she feel that she was able to survive? Meaning to ask her whether or not she was able to survive in a world without Dan, I heard myself say instead, "Are you *willing* to survive in a world without Dan?" Shaking her head no, for the first time she began to cry.

Slowly she began to speak about her loss, the loss of her

dream, the loss of her life companion, the emptiness that seemed never to ease. She uncovered her unwillingness to live without him and her feelings of shame and weakness about this. How could she be unwilling to live when Dan had wanted to live so much? For the first time she broke through her numbness and began to suffer, and so she could now begin to heal. Over the next several sessions I listened as she spoke of the pain she had hidden even from herself.

Finally, I suggested that it was possible that she had not chosen to stop her life but that it had just stopped, in the same way that the shock of diving into cold water causes us to automatically hold our breath. She had suffered a great shock. Perhaps the important thing here was to know her power to choose. She could choose to continue to "circle the wagons" or she could choose another way.

Two weeks later she returned, filled with excitement, saying that she had had a dream. In this dream she was sitting on the ground in the company of a circle of Indians. These were all men and she described them as "the elders." She seemed to know that they had come together to talk to her about stopping her life, to have a council, a sort of fact-finding session. Without speaking they asked her to tell them the story of Dan's death, not in words but in pictures in her mind which they would be able to see. She then began to tell them the story in pictures and they accompanied her as she relived the inner experience of the death of her beloved. The elders paid a great deal more attention to the pictures and the experience, moment to moment, than she had been able to do alone. In their company she was able to find the very moment when she stopped her life.

It was the moment when the men from the undertakers had carried the body of her beloved past her and out of her house.

The group of Indians had sat in silence contemplating this moment together. In this silence she realized that the undertakers were taking him away from her, and that she had stopped life at this moment to prevent them from taking him away.

The group contemplated this new truth with patience and care. She could feel the compassion for her loss surrounding her, see it in every face. And then she knew that with the terrible strength with which she had stopped life to prevent losing Dan, she could choose to let him go. That she was strong enough to live life. That it was time to give him back.

In her dream, the scene shifted. She was walking toward the edge of a high place with Dan's lifeless body in her arms, which seemed to have no weight at all. She somehow knew that she had carried it a long way. When she reached the edge, she lifted him up to let him go. He seemed to become a great bird and as he flew up she could feel a rush of freedom, like a wind, go past her.

Freedom may come not from being in control of life but rather from a willingness to move with the events of life, to hold on to our memories but let go of the past, to choose, when necessary, the inevitable. We can become free at any time.

ATTACHED OR COMMITTED 2

When I was a medical student, an elderly woman came for consultation about a mass on the side of her jaw. Our hospital was one of the leading hospitals for cancer treatment in the world, and the mass was skillfully identified, classed, and staged and state-of-the-art therapy was determined which involved both chemotherapy and the total removal of her lower jaw.

One of the staff doctors went to discuss our findings and recommendations with the woman and her family and schedule the surgery. He returned outraged. The old woman had refused surgery and her family had supported her in this decision. He had explained carefully the almost certain fatal outcome of her sort of cancer without surgery, described the surgery in detail, and given her the statistics of postoperative survival. The old woman had thanked him for his concern and said that she would go home now. All his arguments had failed to move her. Finally he asked her to sign a paper absolving the hospital and staff of all responsibility for the outcome. Calmly, with her family looking on, she had signed. Others had gone to talk with them and with her. Despite enormous pressure from the staff, she left the hospital. She never returned.

Her refusal to accept our help left the staff angry for days. Our attitude effectively disenfranchised her with respect to her own life, yet any of us would have passionately defended her right to vote. Despite her enormous dignity, and the obvious love of her family, I remember thinking that they were very strange people. I never found out what lay behind her choice, what had caused her to make her difficult decision with such calm certainty.

But thirty-five years have brought some change not only to me but to medicine itself. Recently, after I presented this story to a class of medical students, a second-year student commented that he felt the problem was that the doctors had known this woman's disease, but not the woman herself. Who was she? he asked. She was elderly. Had anyone found out what she had lived by all that time? What was important to her?

A fine discussion ensued about the difference between defending a person against death and making a commitment to their life. The students raised some hard questions: How do we serve life? Can we know what is "best" for people, or do we only know what is best for the treatment of their diseases? Is it possible to improve someone's physical health and yet diminish their integrity?

The class split right down the middle. Some felt much the

way that my own classmates had felt, frustrated, judgmental, and angry. But others thought that the doctors of long ago had diagnosed, but they hadn't understood. They had been rendered impotent not by the woman's refusal of surgery but by their own refusal to listen and know who she was. This group of students conceived the task of her doctors not as prolonging her life at all costs but as enabling her to live her life according to her own values. Depending on who she was, this might include prolonging her life or it might not.

I wonder how these comments might have been received thirty-five years ago by my classmates and teachers. I suspect not well. Unquestionably we had missed an opportunity to learn about something far more important than the diagnosis and treatment of cancer, but the capacity to recognize that opportunity lay far in the future.

ALL OR NOTHING

It is actually difficult to edit life. Especially in regard to feelings. Not being open to anger or sadness usually means being unable to be open to love and joy. The emotions seem to operate with an all-or-nothing switch. I never cease to be impressed by the capacity of some ill people to live life more fully than most, to find more meaning and more depth, more awe in the ordinary. Perhaps it is because they have allowed the events of their lives to take them to some extraordinary highs and lows. Meeting people there is a choice.

One of the most challenging people I have treated was a woman with ovarian cancer. In her early sixties, she had lived an extraordinary life, meeting and making opportunities with zest. At one time she had taken her three small children out of school and traveled alone with them around the world. A Zorba the Greek kind of woman.

The cancer and its treatment were more than a match for her exuberance if not her spirit. At first the chemotherapy had claimed only her hair and she appeared in my office, laughing, totally bald with huge exotic earrings. Ultimately, I appeared in her bedroom when she was so weak she could barely open her eyes.

Throughout this whole dreadful experience, she wore a Walkman playing what she called her "chemotherapy music." At first she wore it only to her treatments. Later she wore it constantly. The cancer experience was unlike anything she had faced before. As she put it, "At the start, I saw myself at the top of a ski run. It was a hellacious run. What I didn't realize was that I would have to make it on my knees." Stripped of her trust in her remarkable physical strength and vitality, she found an even greater trust in other, more hidden parts of herself. And she survived.

About a year after the end of her treatment, when her hair and her weight and her laugh had returned, she threw a party for the people who had helped her in her healing. We gathered in her living room, almost one hundred strong, to eat and drink and meet one another. Partway through the evening, she called for silence. Standing on a chair, she spoke of the past two years, her pain, her losses, her hopelessness and despair. We had each been there with her in some way and she thanked us. With a twinkle in her eye she held up a tape and reminded us of her chemotherapy music. She told us it was a single piece of music that she had listened to over and over all those months. She would play it for us now.

With a little start I realized that I had no idea what was on that tape. Dropping it into her hi-fi, she turned the volume high. After a few seconds of silence a voice filled with emotion shouted out, *"Praise God, brothers and sisters!"* and a blast of gospel music rocked the room. There was a moment of shock. Then a hundred people—friends and neighbors, sons, daughters, beauticians, lovers, grocery delivery boys and taxi drivers, masseuses and yoga teachers, nurses, cooks, and house cleaners—began to dance. We danced for a long time. It was one of the great life celebrations I have ever experienced.

As a physician, I was trained to occupy the middle ground, to participate in neither the disappointments nor the hopes of ill people. To be objective. To stand next to life.

Often the price of such a stance is high.

While I was still in medical school, I attended the retirement dinner of one of our faculty members. The recipient of numerous professional prizes, this doctor, well into his seventies, was internationally known and respected for his research and his contributions to medical science. People had come from all over the world to honor him. It was a memorable evening.

The talk he gave was memorable too. With a characteristic brilliance, he summarized the progress of medical science in the fifty years since he had become a physician, integrating it into a stunning synthesis and pointing to the directions of future research. It was an intellectual *tour de force* and he received a long standing ovation.

Later in the evening a group of medical students went to speak to him and offer him our congratulations and admiration. He was gracious. One of our number asked him if he had any words for us now at the beginning of our careers, anything he thought we should know. He hesitated. But then he told us that despite his professional success and recognition he felt he knew nothing more about life now than he had at the beginning. That he was no wiser. His face became withdrawn, even sad. "It has slipped through my fingers," he said.

None of us understood what he meant. Talking about it afterwards, I attributed it to modesty. Some of the others wondered if he had at last become senile. Now, almost thirty-five years later, my heart goes out to him.

EMBRACING LIFE

I HAD ALWAYS assumed that a hospital was a healing environment. The first twenty years of my work with sick people was in hospitals, and by the time my training was complete I had worked in hospitals all over the United States. All hospitals look, feel, and even smell the same. Once you are inside a hospital you cannot tell whether you are in Maine or in Mississippi. I had always thought that this was an example of high standards and quality control. I now know that it is the reflection of the lack of connection between most hospital environments and the natural world around them. This sort of disconnection from the natural world weakens everyone.

In 1988, during my last surgery, every plant that anyone brought to me in the hospital died. Day by day I would watch these plants dying all around me and worry: If plants could not seem to make it here, was this a good place for me to be?

As a physician I am used to working without much support from the natural environment. This year when I was invited to give Psychiatry Rounds at the county hospital, this came up in the discussion. The Rounds were exciting as two radically different ways of helping became clear: the psychiatric approach, which lies within a traditional medical model emphasizing drug therapy, transference, and expertise and my own wounded healer, level-playing-field approach learned from people with cancer whose emotional and physical pain were intertwined.

After the Rounds, I met with the fourteen dedicated young doctors in the training program for a two-hour discussion. They immediately pointed out that the approach which had proved so helpful with people with cancer violated almost every rule of transference that they were learning in their training. I touched patients, hugged them even. My patients knew about me personally, about my own illness and vulnerability and many other details of my life. We ate together. We even cried together. The interpersonal distance that the young doctors had been taught was essential to being of help was simply not there between me and my patients.

Listening carefully as they talked about transference, I realized that they had been trained to create for each patient a meticulous interpersonal environment, a carefully controlled relationship radically different from any other, in which they were personally invisible and their comments and behaviors were calculated and repressed. I could sense the great discipline the training required and feel their fear of inadvertently making a mistake and causing harm. Yet in my experience most relationships have what I can only call a natural poetic value. Often we are unaware of the many levels of symbolism and meaning in interactions as simple as giving a thirsty person a drink or moving over to make room for someone else to sit on a bench. The unconscious mind is always eavesdropping on our relationships and we are often unaware of the messages and meta-messages that translate themselves to another person in our presence. Sometimes the messages we convey unawares may be even more coherent and relevant to the needs of others than the messages we consciously devise.

From transference, the discussion veered off in the direction of the work environment. A resident physician commented that it was probably not possible to establish genuine healing relationships without the natural environment of Commonweal, which is situated on the cliffs above the Pacific in Northern California. He referred to our present location as an example. We were sitting at a long table in a room whose tiny windows were so close to the twenty-foot ceiling that it was impossible to tell the weather or the time of day. The residents laughed and someone commented that at least there were windows.

At this point, a woman physician seated opposite me at the head of the long table spoke for the first time. She described her office, which like all the residents' offices was a room without windows. After the first few weeks in this office the environment had begun to trouble her and so she had brought in a plant. The plant had died. Challenged, she bought another one and a few grow lights. This time she was successful and the plant took hold. In fact, it had done so well that she had repotted it and gotten a couple more. Now there were several plants, some quite large, growing in her office.

All this has had an odd effect on many of her patients, she told us. From the beginning, people seemed to take a great interest in the plants and some were upset when the first one died. The success of the new plant aroused a lot of interest too. Patients would look over at the plant when they first sat down, and many commented on how well it was doing. After a while a few of the patients would pause before sitting to touch a leaf or feel the soil. Encouraged by their interest, she had gotten some small gardening tools and plant food and often would spend the first few minutes of a session talking about the plants and tending them together with her patient.

As the plants grew and her office became a veritable jungle, many patients seemed surprisingly gratified. Some asked if they could take cuttings home. She worried about this a little but then she thought, "Why not?" and many patients now had cuttings. With obvious pleasure they would tell her how well the cuttings were doing. She was aware that this was an unusual thing to be doing, but somehow it had felt right.

Traditionally speaking, this departure from psychiatric protocol was radical but the poetic metaphor was exquisite. I looked around and realized that no one seemed to have recognized the power of it.

Yet every patient is there because in some way they live in a psychological environment that makes growth difficult. Emotionally speaking, they are trying to find a way to live in a room without windows. A windowless office is, in a sense, the perfect meeting place.

All patients come with the same hope: Can the doctor help? In her willingness to slip the constraints of transference she had, unawares, set up the ultimate transference. Her patients find her tending a plant in a place that is hostile to growth. Week by week they watch it growing. They begin to hope. Perhaps there is a way to tend life, a way to grow despite difficulties and limitations. Perhaps she can help them.

After a time they begin to trust her with their pain and allow her to tend the life in them. Gradually they become stronger, more able to participate. Tentatively at first, they join her in tending life. In a while they feel ready to try to take home what they have learned here. They take home a piece of the life they have tended together and find that they can sustain it. Eventually they may not need to come back. I was deeply moved by the wisdom in her story.

Thinking back, I remember that I too once had a plant as a cotherapist. The patient was a remarkable woman who was referred to me because of depression and anxiety. The owner of an interior design firm, she was welcome in the social scene of three continents, on friendly terms with some of the most wild and creative people in the contemporary world. Yet she had come because of a deep loneliness and a long string of self-destructive behaviors and relationships with men. She was a big woman of great warmth and humor and had one of the most wonderful laughs I have ever heard.

Born in Ireland of a socially prominent Catholic family, she was raised in a traditional home in which she had felt safe and protected. As a girl she attended Catholic schools and traveled in the most conservative and proper circles. It had been a pleasant and comfortable life.

"When did all that change?" I asked her. Painfully, she told me of an evening when she had left her boarding school on an errand and been raped at knifepoint. She had received little real support from her overwhelmed parents or her church, who dealt with her shame by covering it over with silence. Shortly afterwards she had left Ireland and moved to the States to live with an aunt.

Although it had happened twenty-five years ago, the rape had left her deeply vulnerable and shamed, unable to set personal boundaries or take control of her life. She took whatever came her way and tried to survive it. She did not believe that she could change things. Yet at work she was powerful and competent, making shrewd decisions and running a successful business in a highly competitive field.

For a year or more we tended the old wounds, raising and healing some unconscious feelings, exploring the conclusions she had drawn about herself and about life. After some months of this we began to examine how she lived her own life. For many years she had spent her life without replenishing or tending it in the company of those who did the same. Telling her that it was my hunch that she had very little experience in caring for her life, I suggested she begin a practice to enable her to learn this. Did I mean meditation? "Not exactly," I said. "Buy a plant." She laughed her wonderful laugh and said that she did not think that she could keep a plant alive. But that was just the point. Dubiously, she agreed to try.

Over the next few months Gert struggled to keep a geranium going. Her task was to pay attention to it every day, noticing its needs and responding to them. At first it was touch and go. The geranium, which was actually a pelargonium, suffered from overindulgence followed by periods of neglect, much like Gert herself. "Listen more carefully," I encouraged her. "If you really pay attention, it will show you what it needs."

Pelargoniums are tenacious. Despite hard times, in the manner of its kind it would recover and continue to grow. Gert began to admire its resilience, to see something of herself in it. She spoke to me about its strength. Gradually she got better at recognizing its needs. Irrepressible as ever, Gert, who spoke four languages fluently, told me that she was learning to speak Pelargonium, and asked if I cared to hear her say something.

We went on to other things. I would inquire about the geranium periodically and eventually Gert said she had to transplant it into the ground as it had outgrown its pot. We were both pleased.

At about this time, Gert began to consider making some changes in her life. The demands of her work were enormous, and she had very little time for herself. Building on a new trust in her judgment and her ability to know what she needed, she sold her business and opened a design school. At about this time, she met a good, kind man and began seeing him. As she moved into this new life and this new relationship, she no longer felt a need for our sessions.

A few years later I received an invitation to her wedding, and a year afterwards she came by to discuss how she might best be helpful to a friend who was dying of cancer. She and her husband are now settled in Los Angeles in their first home. Proudly she showed me pictures. The garden, a riot of color, was enormous. When I commented on its beauty, she grinned. "I planted it myself."

Carl Jung sometimes worked with his patients by asking them where they had been just before they came to the office. Often they had been caught up in the most mundane and ordinary of activities, shopping for food, driving a car, buying shoes. By carefully listening to the way in which they had done these things, asking thoughtful questions and uncovering automatic and habitual responses, Jung would clarify a person's entire way of living, its strengths and limitations.

I have come to suspect that the subjective world is probably a hologram and the pattern of our most fundamental beliefs is reflected in the smallest of our behaviors. If this is so, breaking up that pattern at any one point may eventually free us from it. The way in which we go to the grocery store may tell us everything about the way in which we live a life. The way we tend the life force in a plant may be the way we tend our own life force. We are exquisitely coherent. Healing requires a certain willingness to hear and respond to life's needs. Gert had never listened to her needs, had not known how to listen. The pelargonium was a better teacher of this sort of thing than I was.

VII.

Live and Help Live

WE ALL CAN influence the life force. The tools and strategies of healing are so innate, so much a part of a common human birthright, that we believers in technology pay very little attention to them. But they have lost none of their power.

People have been healing each other since the beginning. Long before there were surgeons, psychologists, oncologists, and internists, we were there for each other. The healing of our present woundedness may lie in recognizing and reclaiming the capacity we all have to heal each other, the enormous power in the simplest of human relationships: the strength of a touch, the blessing of forgiveness, the grace of someone else taking you just as you are and finding in you an unsuspected goodness.

Everyone alive has suffered. It is the wisdom gained from our wounds and from our own experiences of suffering that makes us able to heal. Becoming expert has turned out to be less important than remembering and trusting the wholeness in myself and everyone else. Expertise cures, but wounded people can best be healed by other wounded people. Only other wounded people can understand what is needed, for the healing of suffering is compassion, not expertise.

While I was still part of the Stanford faculty, I was one of a small group of traditional physicians and psychologists invited to a day-long master's class with Dr. Carl Rogers, a pioneering humanistic psychotherapist. I was young and proud of being an expert, sought after for my opinions and judgments. Rogers's approach to therapy, called Unconditional Positive Regard, seemed to me to be a deplorable lowering of standards. Yet it was rumored that his therapeutic outcomes were little short of magical. I was curious and so I went.

Rogers was a deeply intuitive man, and as he spoke to us about how he worked with his patients, he paused often to put into words what he did instinctively and naturally. Very different from the articulate and authoritative style of presentation I was accustomed to at the medical center. Could someone so seemingly hesitant have any expertise at all? I doubted it. From what I could gather, Unconditional Positive Regard came down to sitting in silence and accepting everything the patient said without judgment or interpretation. I could not imagine how this might prove helpful.

Finally, Dr. Rogers offered us a demonstration of his approach. One of the doctors in the class volunteered to act as his client and they rearranged their chairs to sit opposite one another. As Rogers turned toward him and was about to begin the demonstration session he stopped and looked thoughtfully at his little audience of experts, myself among them. In the brief silence, I shifted impatiently in my chair. Then Rogers began to speak. "Before every session I take a moment to remember my humanity," he told us. "There is no experience that this man has that I cannot share with him, no fear that I cannot understand, no suffering that I cannot care about, because I too am human. No matter how deep his wound, he does not need to be ashamed in front of me. I too am vulnerable. And because of this, *I am enough.* Whatever his story, he no longer needs to be alone with it. This is what will allow his healing to begin."

The session that followed was profound. Rogers conducted

it without saying a single word, conveying to his client simply by the quality of his attention a total acceptance of him exactly as he was. The doctor began to talk and the session rapidly became a great deal more than the demonstration of a technique. In the safe climate of Rogers's total acceptance, he began to shed his masks, hesitantly at first and then more and more easily. As each mask fell, Rogers welcomed the one behind it unconditionally, until finally we glimpsed the beauty of the doctor's naked face. I doubt that even he himself had ever seen it before. By that time many of our own faces were naked and some of us had tears in our eyes. I remember wishing that I had volunteered, envying this doctor the opportunity to be received by someone in such a total way. Except for those few moments with my godfather, I had never experienced that kind of welcome.

I had always worked hard at being good enough; it was the golden standard by which I decided what to read, what to wear, how to spend time, where to live, and even what to say. Even "good enough" was not really good enough for me. I had spent a lifetime trying to make myself perfect. But if what Rogers was saying was true, perfection was the booby prize. What was needed was simply to be human. I was human. All my life I had feared being found out.

What Rogers was pointing to is, of course, a very wise and basic principle of healing relationship. Whatever the expertise we have acquired, the greatest gift we bring to anyone who is suffering is our wholeness.

Listening is the oldest and perhaps the most powerful tool of healing. It is often through the quality of our listening and not the wisdom of our words that we are able to effect the most profound changes in the people around us. When we listen, we offer with our attention an opportunity for wholeness. Our listening creates sanctuary for the homeless parts within the other person. That which has been denied, unloved, devalued by themselves and by others. That which is hidden.

In this culture the soul and the heart too often go homeless.

Listening creates a holy silence. When you listen generously to people, they can hear truth in themselves, often for the first time. And in the silence of listening, you can know yourself in everyone. Eventually you may be able to hear, in everyone and beyond everyone, the unseen singing softly to itself and to you.

Not long ago I was walking in the rain in the place where I was born, New York City, thinking of the green place where I now live, grateful for the ease with which things grow there. Not all things have room to grow and fulfill themselves. The rain made me intensely aware of the hardness and grayness of this world of cement and brick and the awesome capacity of human beings to prevail over what is natural and bend it to their will. For miles and miles there seemed to be nothing living that could respond to the rain. But the important thing is that the rain comes. The possibility of growth is there even in the hardest of times. Listening is like the rain.

HUMAN BEING

IN THE BEGINNING of December the year I was thirteen, my father declared bankruptcy. That was the year we all made our Christmas presents. I remember waiting for Christmas with more than the usual anticipation, anxious to know if the muffler I had secretly knit for my father would please him and how the bracelet I had designed and made from copper wire would look on Mom. Despite the stress in the household, on Christmas morning the living room was much as always, the familiar decorations out and the coffee table heaped with presents, only wrapped this year in the sporting green section of the newspaper and tied with last year's red ribbon. Among them lay a small velvet box.

Even at thirteen, I knew that such a box was not likely to contain something homemade. I looked at it with suspicion. My father smiled. "It's for you," he told me. "Open it."

Inside were a pair of twenty-four-karat gold earrings. They were exquisite. I stared at them in silence, bewildered, feeling the weight of my homeliness, my shyness, my hopeless difference from my classmates who easily joked and flirted and laughed. "Aren't you going to try them on?" prompted my father, so I took them into the bathroom, closed the door, and put them on my ears. Cautiously I looked into the mirror. My sallow, pimply face and lank hair, oily before it even dried from a shower, looked much as always. The earrings looked absurd.

Tearing them from my ears, I rushed back into the living room and flung them on the floor. "How could you do this?" I shrieked at my father. "Why are you making fun of me? Take them back. They look stupid. I'm too ugly to wear them. How could you waste all this money?" Then I burst into tears. My father said nothing until I had cried myself out. Then he passed me his clean, folded handkerchief. "I know they don't look right now," he said quietly. "I bought them because someday they will suit you perfectly."

I am truly grateful to have survived my adolescence. At some of its lowest moments, I would get out the box and look at the earrings. My father had spent a hundred dollars he did not have because he believed in the person I was becoming. It was something to hold on to.

Behind my father's gift lay the kind of double vision which is the mark of every healer. He could have told me not to cry, that someday I would be a lovely woman. But that would have belittled my pain and invalidated my experience, the truth of the moment. What he did was far more powerful. He acknowledged my pain and its appropriateness while backing my process. His belief that change would emerge, naturally, in the course of things made all the difference. Wholeness was just a matter of time.

"Human being" is more a verb than a noun. Each of us is unfinished, a work in progress. Perhaps it would be most accurate to add the word "yet" to all our assessments of ourselves and each other. Jon has not learned compassion . . . yet. I have not developed courage . . . yet. It changes everything. I have seen the "yet" become real even at the very edge of life. If life is process, all judgments are provisional. We can't judge something until it is finished. No one has won or lost until the race is over.

"Broken" may be only a stage in a process. A bud is not a broken rose. Only lifeless things are broken. Perhaps the unique process which is a human being is never over. Even at death.

In our instinctive attachments, our fear of change, and our wish for certainty and permanence, we may undercut the impermanence which is our greatest strength, our most fundamental identity. Without impermanence, there is no process. The nature of life is change. All hope is based on process.

At the time of my father's gift, I was profoundly judgmental about most things. What was lacking always seemed so clear to me, and colored my reactions to myself and those around me. I have struggled to free myself from this way of seeing but I never have. Gradually, I have grown to recognize the gift in it, that what I once saw as deficiency is simply the growing edge of things, the places where we need one another and can join together in becoming more whole.

It has taken me somewhat longer to recognize that a diagnosis is simply another form of judgment. Naming a disease has limited usefulness. It does not capture life or even reflect it accurately. Illness, on the other hand, is a process, like life is.

Much in the concept of diagnosis and cure is about fixing, and a narrow-bore focus on fixing people's problems can lead to denial of the power of their process. Years ago, I took full credit when people became well; their recovery was testimony to my skill and knowledge as a physician. I never recognized that without their biological, emotional, and spiritual process which could respond to my interventions, nothing could have changed at all. All the time I thought I was repairing, I was collaborating.

As a pediatrician, I once gave a talk on health to a group of schoolchildren. I had come prepared to talk about the importance of brushing your teeth and not eating junk food, but the children wanted to ask questions that were more important to them. Such things as, "Where do I go when I go to sleep?" and, "Do dead people become angels?" They quickly established the limits of my expertise and then, of course, lost interest in me.

We were meeting outside on the lawn of their school. One little boy, pointing to a yellow flower growing in the grass, asked me, "What's that?" A chorus of voices answered, "A dandelion!" Pointing to a bunch of leaves, he demanded, "And that?"

"A dandelion too!" the voices cried. An older child got up and picked one of the many fluff balls that dotted the lawn. "So then what's this?" he asked, laughing and blowing it away.

"A dandelion!" the voices shouted with glee. A fine existential argument broke out which quickly became heated. Which one was *really* the dandelion? After a few minutes of debate the issue was neatly resolved by one of the oldest children, an adolescent girl. In a superior and bored tone of voice she chided the others for being silly. "It's all a dandelion," she said. "A dandelion is just something that is happening at a place in the world."

And, I suppose, so are we all.

Seeing the life force in human beings brings medicine closer to gardening than to carpentry. I don't fix a rosebush. A rosebush is a living process, and as a student of that process, I can learn to prune, to nurture and cooperate with it in ways that allow it best to "happen," to maximize the life force in it even in the presence of disease.

Simply trusting process has a great power. A colleague was telling me about the birth of her grandchild. At one point in a long and difficult labor, her daughter had called out to her for help. My colleague experienced this as a moment of impotence, feeling that there was nothing that she could do to fix things. She had sat there holding her child's hand, trusting the process of birth and feeling that this was not enough. But perhaps it is. The trust of process that comes from personal knowledge and experience is really the foundation of helping and comforting one another. Without it all of our actions are driven by fear. Fear is the friction in all transitions.

LIVE AND HELP LIVE

MANY YEARS AGO when I was a teaching pediatrician at a major medical school, I followed six young teenagers with juvenile diabetes. Most of them had diabetes since they were toddlers and had responsibly followed strict diets and given themselves injections of insulin since kindergarten. But as they became caught up in the turmoil of adolescence, desperate to be like their peer group, this disease had become a terrible burden, a mark of difference. Youngsters who had been in diabetic control since infancy now rebelled against the authority of their disease as if it were a third parent. They forgot to take their shots, ate whatever the gang ate, and were brought to the emergency room in coma or in shock, over and over again. It was frightening and frustrating, dangerous for the youngsters and draining for their parents and the entire pediatric staff.

As the associate director of the clinics, this problem was brought to my door and I decided to try something simple. I formed two discussion groups, each consisting of three youngsters and the parents of the other three. Each group met to talk once a week.

These groups turned out to be very powerful. Kids who could not talk to their own parents became articulate in expressing their needs and perspectives to the parents of other children. Parents who could not listen to their own children hung on every word of other people's children. And other people's children could hear them when they could not hear their own parents. People, feeling themselves understood for the first time, felt safe enough to cry and found that others cared and could comfort them. People of all ages offered each other insights and support, and behaviors began to change. Parents and their own children began to talk and listen to each other in new ways. We were making great progress in the quality of all the family relationships, and the number of emergency room visits was actually diminishing, when the director of the clinics discovered the groups.

His indignation was painful. What was I thinking of to overstep the limitations of my expertise in such a blatant way? Was I a psychiatrist? What if one of these people had gotten hurt by something that was said, or had become emotionally disturbed? What would I have done then? Despite the good results, the groups were disbanded.

There is still a very narrow conception of what a health provider is. Thinking back on those people and the wisdom, kindness, and understanding they offered each other, I am sad.

They were not second-class experts. And having been ill since adolescence, neither was I. Our life experience was as valuable as any credential.

I do not think that we will be able to attain health for all until we realize that we are all providers of each other's health, and value what we have to offer each other as much as what experts have to offer us. In the years since, groups such as these have demonstrated beyond question that problems which are not amenable to the most expert medical approaches may be resolved in community by the very people who suffer from them and therefore understand them. In such communities, the concept of woundedness breaks down and we are all wounded healers of each other. We have earned the wisdom to heal and the ability to care.

In a recent talk, Bill Moyers commented that one of the most traditional values of the American way of life—live and let live—can never establish good health for all. Health requires us as individuals and as a people to go a step beyond this. To live and *help* live.

HOW WE SEE ONE ANOTHER

As an adolescent I was tall, pimply, and frankly homely. My family is a family of elegant women and my second cousin, who was several years older than I, took it upon herself to help me with the graces that my intellectual parents deemed unimportant. One Saturday a month she would take me shopping and then to lunch at the Russian Tea Room, a formal and lovely place in New York. These excursions were agony for me. All the clothes I tried on hung on me. I had grown tall rapidly and was painfully clumsy. Once I tripped over my own feet and fell full-length in the street, scraping both knees and my chin and soiling my dress. My cousin was a very kind woman who seemed neither critical nor ashamed of me. She helped me up and took me to tea, bleeding chin, dirty dress, and all.

After a few years of this she married. Caught up in the demands of my education and then my professional training, I lost touch with her. Some years later, when her children were in school and I was a young doctor, we resumed our shopping lunches. Now when we entered the Russian Tea Room together, we would stop conversation. The both of us very tall and exotic-looking, we would take it by storm. This might have been great fun except for the fact that my cousin had never updated her inner picture of me. Despite the obvious changes in my looks and capabilities, she still saw me as a hopelessly clumsy adolescent. And I could not escape her unspoken expectations.

We would sit down to lunch and in the course of the afternoon I would regress. I would spill my red wine across the flawless white tablecloth or dribble gravy down the front of my dress. Once the strap of my purse caught underneath the bag, upsetting it and spilling lipsticks, keys, wallets, and tampons across the tearoom floor. My cousin bore these incidents graciously without comment. Totally unaware of her role in these happenings and the power of her private image, she would smile at me with compassion and acceptance and help me clean up the mess. It was infuriating.

We are, in a certain way, defined as much by our potential as by its expression. There is a great difference between an acorn and a little bit of wood carved into an acorn shape, a difference not always readily apparent to the naked eye. The difference is there even if an acorn never has the opportunity to plant itself and become an oak. Remembering its potential changes the way in which we think of an acorn and react to it. How we value it. If an acorn were conscious, knowing its potential would change the way that it might think and feel about itself. The Hindus use the greeting *"Namaste"* instead of our more noncommittal "Hello." The connotation of this is roughly, "Whatever your outer appearance, I see and greet the soul in you." There is a wisdom in such ways of relating. Sometimes we can best help other people by remembering that what we believe about them may be reflected back to them in our presence and may affect them in ways we do not fully understand.

Perhaps a sense of possibility is communicated by our tone of voice, facial expression, or a certain choice of words. Over the years I have come to wonder if it may even be communicated more directly, by the sharing of a private image in a mysterious yet tangible way, as my cousin did with me.

Holding and conveying a sense of possibility does not mean making demands or having expectations. It may mean having no expectations, but simply being open to whatever promise the situation may hold and remembering the inability of anyone to know the future. Thoreau said that we must awaken and stay awake not by mechanical means, but by a constant expectation of the dawn. There's no need to demand the dawn, the dawn is simply a matter of time. And patience. And the dawn may look quite different from the story we tell ourselves about it. My experience has shown me the wisdom of remaining open to the possibility of growth in any and all circumstances, without ever knowing what shape that growth may take.

When people are ill, our private image of them may have more far-reaching consequences than we realize.

I met Aaron, a young architect, when he was being seen at

the university hospital for treatment of lymphoma. A bear of a man, with supreme confidence in his physical strength, he was brought down for the first time by the power of the chemotherapy. A lesser man would have been bedridden, but Aaron somehow managed to see his clients and drive himself fifty miles to the hospital for his treatments. During our sessions he spoke often of the young doctor, the oncology fellow, who had been assigned to him. Virtually the same age, the two men had begun to talk beyond the diagnosis and treatment, about their dreams and their values. Gradually their relationship had become important to Aaron; he felt that his doctor saw him not just as a patient but as a man.

The chemotherapy continued for a year. I marveled at Aaron's determination, the power of his wish to live. When the treatment was finally over, he and his young wife and children began to rebuild the quality of their life together. Aaron's strength returned quickly. Soon he was once again coaching Little League, backpacking in the Sierra, and beating his friends into submission on the tennis courts. He continued to do well for two years.

During this time, the oncology fellow left to take additional training, preparing himself to specialize further. He returned to complete his fellowship and Aaron saw him for the first time in two years during a routine checkup. Delighted, Aaron invited him to join his wife and himself for a night on the town. The two young couples could have dinner and perhaps see a play. The young doctor hesitated. Awkwardly he said that he didn't think this would be a good idea. Puzzled, Aaron asked, "Why not?" The doctor became even more uneasy. "Well," he mumbled, "I don't want to get too close, I need to protect myself. After all, you have cancer."

Aaron was devastated. Over the next few months he could talk of nothing else in his sessions. Despite my best efforts, I was unable to convince him that his doctor trusted the efficacy of his therapy and believed in the possibility that Aaron could beat his disease. He became depressed. I called his physician, who dismissed my concern as fanciful. After all, he had simply told Aaron honestly how he felt. "We all know the odds."

"People do beat those odds," I reminded him.

"Not often," he replied.

Four months later, Aaron's disease recurred. A bone marrow transplant was attempted, but he did not survive. I received a long summary letter from his physician in which he mentioned his deep respect and admiration for the way in which Aaron had handled his disease and his life, and commented on the benefits of the psychological work we had done. I have had several referrals from this doctor over the years.

I continue to remember the impact of his doctor's words on Aaron and wonder if they affected more than his mood. Traditional medical belief would suggest this is not the case and no rigorous scientific studies exist that indicate the contrary, yet thinking back on the Russian Tea Room, I am not sure. Certainly Aaron's doctor did not see his own attitude as a force in his patient's outcome. Yet is this so surprising? Most of us don't realize the extent of our influence on others and the potential of our inner world of attitude and belief to affect them. It's just not part of our culture.

I once experienced something of this sort as a patient. Because I had not seen a doctor for some time, I set up a consultation with Dr. Z., a recognized expert in Crohn's disease, to see if any new approaches had been developed. I sent him a forty-page summary of my extensive medical and surgical records and then we spoke on the phone directly. Between his schedule and mine, we were not able to find a meeting time for more than two months.

Dr. Z. had a formal and traditional office. His consulting room, filled with medical texts and journals, was dominated by a huge desk. He sat on one side of this in his white coat and indicated a chair to me on the other side. Across a very large stretch of mahogany, he began to ask me a series of questions about my present condition. What medications was I taking? What symptoms did I have? His questions were careful and thoughtful. My answers were the same. Then unexpectedly he asked me a truly wonderful question. "Tell me the story of your illness from the beginning," he said. In all these years, no one had ever asked me this question before. "It's very long," I told him. "Fine," he replied.

So I began my story, which involved years of intensive therapy with toxic drugs, several major surgical procedures, and many dramatic happenings, such as being in coma after a massive bleed at the beginning of my disease, growing a full beard at sixteen and needing to shave every day from the impure cortisone which was all that was available for treatment, starting new drugs while in college and coming home at Thanksgiving so altered in appearance that my father did not recognize me at the airport until I spoke his name, having such severe bone loss during the ten years I was treated with high-dose cortisone therapy that once or twice a bone spontaneously fractured in the midst of the most ordinary of circumstances.

I went on, including a near-death experience—in the midst of a surgery—and the loss of a significant part of my vision from steroid-induced cataracts and glaucoma. I had never put it all together like this before and the effect was just overwhelming. I also spoke of the inexplicable lessening of the symptoms, so that my present problems were not the result of the disease but of some of the procedures and medications of long ago, long range effects my early doctors never expected me to live to experience. "It had me," I told him, "but it let me go."

It took almost forty-five minutes to tell all this and he listened attentively without interrupting. When I was finished, he leaned forward and in a kind voice asked me if I was still able to practice medicine a little. Shocked, I reminded him that I was about as busy as he was. He seemed acutely embarrassed then and changed the subject.

But his remark had reawakened a deep sense of doubt. Many years ago, other doctors had told me that I would be dead long before now. On the strength of their authority I had decided not to marry or become a parent. If this man, so expert in the management of my disease, felt that in my situation I could not possibly be an active and contributing member of society, was there any reason to suppose that I might not become an invalid tomorrow? Or the next day? Did my life, as I knew it, have any security? Could it be trusted? The power of the expert is very great and the way in which an expert sees you may easily become the way in which you see yourself.

In the weeks following this visit, I began to worry over

many of the physical problems I had lived with comfortably for years. I even canceled some talks I was scheduled to give on the East Coast because I did not feel secure about being three thousand miles away from doctors who knew my case. Finally one of my friends asked me why I seemed to be having such a hard time. Almost in tears, I told him what had happened. "May I hear the story too?" he asked, and so I told it again. Like Dr. Z., my friend listened thoughtfully, without interrupting, but he heard something very different. When I had finished he looked at me for a long time. "God, Rachel, I had no idea. You *are* a warrior!" he said, and healed me.

TOUCHING

In one of the morning sessions I lead during our cancer retreats the participants do a form of hands-on healing with each other. Most of the other morning group leaders do this with their groups as well. I started doing this in hopes of putting people more in touch with their own capacity to heal. Most people who come to these retreats have been on the receiving end of things for a long time. It can make a person feel small, broken, and vulnerable. Here, no matter how sick they are, people have a chance to offer healing to each other and can sometimes recognize the strength of the healing force in themselves for the first time.

The hands-on healing session has been a time of discovery for many people. Few of us have had the opportunity to touch and be touched in this way. For many it is very moving, an experience of genuine intimacy. People talk about how different others look to them afterwards. They often speak of their feelings of reverence for the life in the person they are partnered with and are surprised by a sense of commitment to that life. Spontaneous images come up which have to do with the healing or the essential nature and wholeness of the person themselves. Many express a sense of gratitude for the opportunity to be together in this way. This is true whether people are religious or not, educated or not, young or old. It is true even when partners have not liked each other before they do this exercise together. As a matter of fact, that often changes after this sort of an experience.

As powerful as these experiences are, they do not begin to approach what happens when this same exercise is done with a group of highly trained medical specialists. Having done this with more than sixty physicians in my institute's training programs at Commonweal, I have found that many of those trained to cure have a deep, innate recognition and understanding of the process of healing.

In medicine, we are not trained to heal directly. For most physicians, touch is a source of information, a major strategy of diagnosis and sometimes of treatment. We are trained to connect hand and mind. Yet after fifteen minutes of explanation and discussion, groups of eight physicians can step past a collective hundred and fifty years of such training and reclaim what seems for many of them to be a more familiar and genuine way of relating to the suffering of others. While it is a great privilege to do this with people with cancer, watching physicians heal each other is one of the most moving things I have witnessed anywhere. It sometimes seems to me as if they are recovering the very meaning of their work and their lives, freeing themselves from generations of distortion and myth to reclaim a deeply recognized integrity. Other physicians are usually as deeply affected by this experience as I am and the insights they gain are often profound.

Many are surprised by how natural it seems to them to sit with someone else in silence and touch them with healing intent. The most commonly made observation is that it feels like something remembered. Some say they have wanted to touch some of their patients in a healing way, but felt that it was not professional or that it would not be welcome.

Like people with cancer, the doctors comment on how unusual it is to be touched by someone who wants only your wellbeing and how rarely they have been touched like this. They often comment that it would take only a simple inner shift to touch someone with healing intent in the very process of doing a routine physical exam.

Many physicians have been surprised to find that they have a deep and intuitive knowledge of each other's wounds. The peace experienced in just meeting with someone's pain without the pressure to fix it is new for most of them. In this setting many have become aware again of how deeply they care. It is a steep learning curve.

Of the many stories which come out of this exercise, my favorite involves a very handsome and intimidating woman physician in her early thirties who is a highly successful general surgeon. The brilliance of her mind and the strength of her will were unusual even for this group. In the discussions, hers was the voice which challenged opinions or questioned the logic of others' ideas. Often she was right but the effect was to create a certain distance. I suspected that this sort of distance lay between herself and life in general.

For the exercise, she found herself paired with a male oncologist. Afterwards, he described the experience this way:

"At first I thought I would just play it safe, but after Jane told me about the pain she usually has in her back I decided to take a chance and tell her about my divorce, which was final last year. How hard it had become for me to trust women. She asked me where I felt this pain and I couldn't actually say it, so I just touched my heart. She nodded. Then I lay down on the rug and closed my eyes and she sat next to me for a little while without touching me. I remember thinking that she probably was not going to touch me and suddenly I felt like crying. I was so surprised; I had not cried through this whole thing. But I didn't cry. Then Jane put the palm of her hand on my chest. I was really astonished by how warm her hand was, and how gently and tenderly she touched me. A little at a time the warmth of her hand seemed to penetrate my chest and surround my heart. I had a sort of strange experience. For a while there, it seemed to me as if she was holding my heart in her hand rather than just touching my chest. That's when I felt the strength in her hand, how rock-steady she was, and in a funny way I could feel that she was really *there* for my pain, committed to being there, and suddenly I felt I was not alone. I was safe. That's when I started to cry." He turned to her and said, "I had no idea who you were. Your patients are lucky."

Jane was close to tears herself. In a halting voice she began to talk about all that she felt she had lost through her medical training—her softness, her gentleness, her warmth. About how there was no approval for these things in the masculine world of medicine and so in an effort to succeed as a physician she had cut them off. The exercise had put her in touch with the pain of this. She had thought these parts of herself had been lost, and it meant a great deal to her to be seen and valued in this way. "The patients never tell you," she said.

By this time it had become clear to every physician in the room that Jane was not just talking about herself or even about other women doctors, she was speaking for all physicians who have been trained to deny their wholeness in the mistaken belief that this would enable them to be of greatest service to others. She was talking about us all.

THE MEETING PLACE

THE PLACES WHERE we are genuinely met and heard have great importance to us. Being in them may remind us of our strength and our value in ways that many other places we may pass through do not.

My medical partner, who had never been ill a day in his life, died suddenly of a massive heart attack at fifty-six. He was a consummate healer and a magnificent friend and he left both his colleagues and his patients bereft. For weeks we numbly went through papers and made referrals for the many people who called in, many of them weeping. Finally, the last details were attended to and we settled down to a future without Hal.

Then the patients started coming. For almost a year afterwards, several times a week I would open the door of my office and find one of Hal's patients sitting in the common waiting room. At first I would worry that they didn't know about Hal and I would have to tell them, but they all knew. They had just come to the place where they had experienced his listening, his special way of seeing and valuing them, just to sit there for a bit, perhaps to think about difficult decisions which currently faced them. Many patients came. It was terribly, terribly moving. It made me angry with Hal for tending every life so impeccably except his own.

Another colleague, who is the head of the department of family medicine at one of the East Coast's outstanding medical schools, tells a story about one of his patients. The patient was a homeless woman whose possessions fit into two shopping carts. Once a month she would bring these up the steep hill to his clinic by lashing them alternately to the parking meters with a belt. First she would tie one, then wheel the other to the next meter uphill, tie it, go back for the first one, untie it, and wheel it to the meter above the second until both she and the two carts were at the clinic's front door. He saw her once a month on a Wednesday. Her speech was sometimes rambling and her clothing was filthy and eccentric. This deeply kind and respectful man was not troubled by this. With his usual grave courtesy he welcomed her into his consulting room, listened to the details of her difficult life, and did what he could to ease her burden.

After he had been seeing her for some time, he became aware that she sometimes came to the hospital on days when he was not there. The clinic nurses were puzzled by this at first, as she seemed to know in some mysterious way that it was not her day to see the doctor. After talking with her, they determined that she simply wanted to go to his consulting room. Once there she did not go in, but would stand on the threshold and slowly and deliberately place her right foot inside the empty room and then withdraw it again and again. After a while she would be satisfied and go away again.

The places in which we are seen and heard are holy places. They remind us of our value as human beings. They give us the strength to go on. Eventually they may even help us to transform our pain into wisdom.

THE HOLY SHADOW

There is a Sufi story about a man who is so good that the angels ask God to give him the gift of miracles. God wisely tells them to ask him if that is what he would wish.

So the angels visit this good man and offer him first the gift of healing by hands, then the gift of conversion of souls, and lastly the gift of virtue. He refuses them all. They insist that he choose a gift or they will choose one for him. "Very well," he replies. "I ask that I may do a great deal of good without ever knowing it." The story ends this way:

The angels were perplexed. They took counsel and resolved upon the following plan: Every time the saint's shadow fell behind him it would have the power to cure disease, soothe pain, and comfort sorrow. As he walked, behind him his shadow made arid paths green, caused withered plants to bloom, gave clear water to dried-up brooks, fresh color to pale children, and joy to unhappy men and women. The saint simply went about his daily life diffusing virtue as the stars diffuse light and the flowers scent, without ever being aware of it. The people respecting his humility followed him silently, never speaking to him about his miracles. Soon they even forgot his name and called him "the Holy Shadow."

It is comforting to think that we may be of help in ways that we don't even realize. One of my own personal healers is probably completely unaware of the difference she made in my life. In fact, I do not know even her name and I am sure she has long forgotten mine.

At twenty-nine, much of my intestine was removed surgically and I was left with an ileostomy. A loop of bowel opens on my abdomen and an ingeniously designed plastic appliance, which I remove and replace every few days, covers it. Not an easy thing for a young woman to live with. While this surgery had given me back much of my vitality, the appliance and the profound change in my body made me feel hopelessly different, permanently shut out of the world of femininity and elegance.

At the beginning, before I could change my appliance myself, it was changed for me by nurse specialists called enterostomal therapists. These white-coated professionals would enter my hospital room, put on an apron, a mask and gloves and then remove and replace my appliance. The task completed, they would strip off all this protective clothing. Then they would carefully wash their hands. This elaborate ritual made things harder for me. I felt shamed.

One day a woman about my age came to do this task. It was

late in the day and she was not dressed in a white coat, but in a silk dress, heels, and stockings. In a friendly way she asked if I was ready to have my appliance changed. When I nodded, she pulled back the covers, produced a new appliance, and in the most simple and natural way imaginable removed my old one and replaced it, without putting on gloves. I remember watching her hands. She had washed them carefully *before* she touched me. They were soft and gentle and beautifully cared for. She was wearing a pale pink nail polish and her rings were gold.

I doubt that she ever knew what her willingness to touch me in such a natural way meant to me. In ten minutes she not only tended my body, but healed my wounds and gave me hope. What is most professional is not always what is most healing.

In the past few years a great deal of attention has been paid to angels and many people have become more aware of the possibility that insight and guidance may be offered at surprising times and in surprising ways. Books have been written about meetings with such celestial messengers and the help and healing they have offered. What is not so commonly recognized is that it is not only angels that carry divine messages of healing and guidance; any one of us may be used in this same way. We are messengers for each other. The difference between us and the folks with the wings is that we often carry these messages without knowing. Like the Holy Shadow.

It has been my experience and the experience of many other therapists that when I am facing a difficult personal issue or a painful decision or am struggling with some recalcitrant and stubborn part of my self, a very peculiar thing will happen. Many of my clients will spontaneously bring in the same issue.

Completely unaware of the personal importance of the issue to me, they will work on some aspect of it as it pertains to them, all the while offering me, through their own work, guidance and perspective on the issue for my healing. Sometimes they work on the very issue or sometimes in the process of working on something else they will offer a single sentence or thought that cuts through my confusion and frees me.

I have many examples of this, but one stands out in my mind. It was a time when I discovered that a friend had incorporated some of my ideas and exercises into her best-selling book without acknowledging where she had learned them. I felt hurt and betrayed by this until my third client of the day sat down and pleasantly remarked, "You know, you can get a lot of good done in this world if you don't care who gets the credit." Astonished, I asked her what had made her think of this. "Oh," she said, "it was on the bumper sticker of the car that just pulled out of my parking spot."

Perhaps the world is one big healing community and we are all healers of each other. Perhaps we are all angels. And we do not know.

Sometimes the message is less direct. Twenty-five years ago I found myself caught between two paradigms. I had been on the faculty of Stanford's medical school for several years but I had become increasingly restless. A number of people had come my way who had knowledge of a different way of doing things: anthropologists, psychologists, artists, messengers from the world beyond medicine, students of another wisdom about pain and suffering. More and more, I found myself participating in discussions of healing rather than curing.

It was 1973 and at the time there was no place for these ideas in medical work or teaching, and yet, as a patient myself, I recognized them and they seemed to me to be of great significance. I began to wonder about certain things. Did people's beliefs about themselves affect their ability to get well? Could people have an intuitive sense of the direction of their healing? Was there more to helping people recover than knowing the right diagnosis and offering the proper treatment? Did our relationship to our patients affect outcome as profoundly as our medications? Slowly, I began to question things that no one around me doubted were true. Over a period of time, I felt myself moving farther and farther away from the perspectives of my colleagues. I was unable to reach across the widening gap in our thinking and it was frightening.

The stress was so severe that I found myself wondering if I could continue in my present work, although there was nowhere to go to work differently. I didn't seem to belong anywhere and I was no longer sure of who I was or what I believed in.

One of my new friends had given me a book of poetry—Khalil Gibran's *The Prophet*—which had in it several illustrations by the poet himself, among them a drawing of a hand with a gentle and compassionate human eye in its palm. I discovered that this was a traditional Hindu symbol for the healer. In the Hindu belief the energy centers called chakras, in our palms, connect the hand and heart of the healer and convey the wisdom and energy needed for the healing. This was in direct contrast to my training, which had led me to place trust in the intellect as the tool of healing. Yet this older idea of being able to "see" with your hands was for some reason compelling to me, and I found myself thinking about it a great deal. It seemed familiar.

Eventually, I took the page from the book and framed it. I felt uncomfortable hanging it in my office at Stanford and so I put it over my desk at home.

The stress continued to build and then I received an unexpected and significant faculty promotion. Amid a flurry of congratulations, I became increasingly troubled. It seemed to me that a choice had to be made, between the path that I had spent half my lifetime preparing to travel—the way to recognition, security, and professional acceptance—and another path, dimly perceived and poorly understood, that led off into the unknown. How could I even consider such an alternative? A hundred other physicians would kill to step into my shoes. I desperately wanted to accept the promotion, but something held me back. I temporized.

At this time I was living on one coast and my family was on the other. A few times a year, I would fly across the country to visit my parents, to New York in the summer and to Florida in the winter. One of these occasions, my thirty-fifth birthday, was coming up. With a heavy heart, I arrived in Florida to spend a week with the family, whose financial sacrifices had made possible my medical training. I knew my promotion would bring them great satisfaction, but somehow I couldn't bring myself to tell them about it.

On my birthday I took a walk with my mother. We sat after a while on a park bench in the Florida sunshine, talking about what she could remember of my birth: I had been born ahead of time by cesarean section. I had been in an incubator for some time. She had felt guilty about this, as if my suffering were her fault. It was very moving for me to hear some things that I had not known, and as I sat listening to her tell me my own story, I remember having the single clear thought that here was the one person who had known me from my very beginnings, who knew who I really was.

Just then my mother turned to look at a young woman sitting on the next bench who was playing with her little girl. The child was drawing little faces on the tips of her fingers with a felt-tip pen and speaking to them as if they were little puppet people. She and her mother were laughing. I was charmed.

After watching for a while in silence, my own mother turned to me with a smile and remarked with some emphasis, "Some things never change."

"Why, what do you mean, Mom?" Delighted with the memory, she told me that when I was small I too used to draw on my hands. I had absolutely no recollection of this and asked her if I had drawn little faces on my fingertips.

"No," my mother said. "You used to do a funny thing. You would take your daddy's fountain pen and draw eyes in the palms of your hands. Then you would hold your hands up on either side of your face with your palms facing forward like this," she said, showing me. "You would close your eyes and say, '*Now* I can see you,' and giggle. Such a funny thing. Sometimes you would not let us wash your hands for days. You were about four. Do you remember now?"

On an average day in the pediatric clinics, I washed my hands thirty or forty times. Perhaps over the years, I had washed away my eyes. About two weeks later, I resigned from Stanford and began searching for my lost eyes.

HEALING IS MUTUAL

One of my patients once defined a healer as someone who can see the movement toward wholeness in you more clearly than you can at any given moment. I remember flying to a medical conference with one of my colleagues. Between San Francisco and Boston, I healed him twice and he healed me three times.

Frank is a middle-aged internist, the director of one of the medical clinics at a midwestern inner-city hospital. For some time now he has secretly thought about leaving medicine for something else, something more satisfying. Someone suggested that he try a physicians' training program I teach before he made any big choices, and for the past nine months he has been reclaiming for himself that which is satisfying in his work. He tells this story about returning to his clinic after a weekend workshop on the power of intuition:

His clinic is at a large teaching hospital. As faculty, part of his job is to see those patients who have no "teaching value." Those who present a medical challenge or a diagnostic problem are saved for the younger doctors who are still in training.

On this particular Monday afternoon, one of these patients, a Mrs. Gonzales, was his regular two o'clock appointment. She was an elderly lady, maybe eighty, in the last stages of breast cancer. No further cancer treatment was available for her, so at each visit he would listen to how her week went, adjust her pain medications, and treat any other complaints she had as best he could.

On this Monday, as always, he made adjustments in her palliative regime and then, thinking of the weekend, he decided to take a few moments to reflect and see what his intuition had to say about her. Much to his surprise, his intuition suggested that what would be most helpful to Mrs. Gonzales now would be for them to pray together.

He was not a praying man and he began to sweat. Professionally, this felt risky to him. He reviewed the danger checklist from the workshop in his mind: Was there some reason not to do this? Would following his intuitive insight cause anyone harm? Would it delay or negate some needed treatment? Would it embarrass or humiliate anyone? Going down the list, he could not find a good reason to discard his insight. So, there it was.

So Frank turned to this ill, grandmotherly patient and said, "Mrs. Gonzales, perhaps it might be good if we prayed together." She looked at him and began to cry.

Fortunately, he didn't do what I had been trained to do years ago when a patient cried. He didn't call a nurse. He did what he had learned to do in another of the training workshops. Taking her hand, he simply received her emotions respectfully and waited. Still holding his hand, she said, "That would be very wonderful, Doctor." Then she told him that she was a Catholic and asked him if they could kneel down. Shaken, he looked toward the door. It was closed. He was on highly unfamiliar ground, but he was in it already and he decided to continue. "Certainly," he replied.

So, in his white coat, he helped her to kneel down and he knelt down with her in the tiny examining room. She began to pray, first in Spanish and then in English. He had not prayed for many years, but a calm settled over him and his memory, awakened by the sound of her voice, gave him back a prayer from his childhood. When she had finished, he said it aloud. There was a long comfortable silence.

Then very gently the old woman reached across and touched his cheek. First in Spanish and then in English she asked God to bless him and strengthen him in doing his important work. He says he can still feel the touch of her hand even six months later. He remembers it when things get tough, and it helps him.

He often prays with his patients now, both for them and for himself.

One of the reasons that many physicians feel drained by their work is that they do not know how to make an opening to receive anything from their patients. The way we were trained, receiving is considered unprofessional. The way most of us were raised, receiving is considered a weakness.

GIVING DARSHAN

Dying people have the power to heal the rest of us in unusual ways. Years afterwards, many people can remember what a dying person has said to them and carry it with them through their lives. Perhaps dying people give a sort of darshan to the rest of us in the same way that spiritual teachers do.

The practice of darshan is very moving. The guru sits before his disciples and throws out a shower of small pieces of candy and glazed fruits, symbolic of the wisdom of his enlightened state. The students who catch the candies eat them and incorporate the sweetness of the guru's wisdom into themselves. The darshan we eat is woven into our fabric, as it were, and becomes a part of who we are.

The sayings and perspectives of a dying person are often carried in this way, woven into our fabric, changing us from then on, helping us to live better.

I carry in this way the death of a woman who in life had never been a close friend. She was outspoken, and somewhat judgmental, and I had found her edge intimidating. Though I admired her work and we traveled in the same circles, I had always kept my distance. Even when I was told she had been diagnosed with cancer, I did not personally call but thought about her and kept in touch with her struggle by calling mutual friends. Our paths had been converging for many years, but I had not known this and so I was surprised when her husband called me to say that Mary was dying and wanted to see me. Uncertain of why she had called, I went.

The woman who welcomed me to her bedroom was no one I had met before. Thin and completely bald, obviously gravely ill, her beauty was magnetic. As gracious as a queen, she patted her bed, indicating that I was to climb in and sit. I remember the four hours that followed as one of the most intimate, strengthening, and healing times I have experienced. We spoke of illness and pain, and she said with simplicity that she was no longer suffering. We spoke of the complexity which had characterized her life and all of her relationships, both family and friends. We told each other jokes. At one point her husband joined us and we read Proverbs 31, A Woman of Valor, together. It was a favorite of hers. Certain of the lines are with me still: "She layeth her hands to the spindle, and her hands hold the distaff." "She is not afraid of the snow for her household, for all her household are clothed with scarlet." We all drank Snapple, rolling it around in our mouths as if it were fine wine.

Part of our discussion turned around the power of this time of dying in a person's life. She had experienced a liberation from some lifelong limitations and self-doubts and felt that she could now reach others in ways not previously possible. She felt grateful for this and for the clarity of vision that seemed to allow her to release her habit of anger and judgment and see the beauty in others. She wondered why this gift had been given her at this time and if it was to be used in some way. I told her that I felt that if it was, she would be shown how to use it. As our time together ended I felt reluctant to go, as if I had been granted an audience with a high lama. But it was only Mary. Eventually she fell asleep in the middle of a sentence and I left.

A few days later, her husband called to say that she had gone into coma, and asked me if I wanted to come and say goodbye. Her house was very still and peaceful. Climbing the stairs to her bedroom, I had the sense of a holy silence that she had somehow drawn around her. Mary lay in her bed in a deep coma, breathing shallowly. I took her hand and sat with her for a while, thinking of our last conversation. Suddenly her eyes were open. They were as clear as a young child's and as honest. In the intensity of her gaze I felt naked, seen in all my particulars and incompleteness. Yet I did not feel embarrassed or even vulnerable. She looked at me in this way for a long while and then she smiled gently and said, "I love you." Closing her eyes, she slipped back into coma.

I have carried the moment with me as a sort of touchstone. Her husband tells me that many of the people who came to see her after she went into coma had experiences similar to mine. She had opened her eyes and met with them in the same singular way, delivering the same last message. In looking back on it, it was a pure moment of intimacy and the power of it is not easily describable. I think of it as a sort of null hypothesis. The null hypothesis is a research principle that applies only when one is studying universal laws and principles, forces that hold in all circumstances and at all times. It states that should one find only a single instance in which the law does not hold, the law itself has been invalidated.

There are laws of our inner world that bind each of us as firmly as gravity, beliefs we carry about ourselves and about life in general that we experience as true in all conditions and at all times. A feeling of personal unworthiness is one such inner law. One moment of unconditional love may call into question a lifetime of feeling unworthy and invalidate it.

Perhaps these final moments with me and the others were a time of healing for Mary as well. After years of anger and self-doubt, the words of Proverbs had finally become true for her. "She perceiveth that her merchandise is good, her candle goeth not out by night."

VIII.

Knowing God

Each person is born with an unencumbered spot, free of expectation and regret, free of ambition and embarrassment, free of fear and worry, an umbilical spot of grace where we were each first touched by God. It is this spot of grace that issues peace. Psychologists call this spot the Psyche, Theologists call it the Soul, Jung calls it The Seat of the Unconscious, Hindu masters call it the Atman, Buddhists call it the Dharma, Rilke calls it Inwardness, Sufis call it Qualb, and Jesus calls it The Center of Our Love.

To know this spot of inwardness is to know who we are, not by surface markers of identity, not by where we work or what we wear or how we like to be addressed but by feeling our place in relation to the Infinite and by inhabiting it. This is a hard lifelong task, for the nature of becoming is a constant filming over of where we begin while the nature of being is a constant erosion of what is not essential. We each live in the midst of this ongoing tension, growing tarnished or covered over only to be worn back to that incorruptible spot of grace at our core.

MARK NEPO

THE SHAMANS attribute illness to soul loss, a loss of a sense of awareness of the sacred in us and around us. Sacred experience is subjective and even intuitive experience. Growing up in this culture, many people have developed and cultivated a harder-edged notion of what is real. Few of us can easily talk about those things we cannot touch or express in numbers, no matter how commonplace the experience. And the experience of God is commonplace. God is in the ordinary, the minute particulars. When you come right down to it, all life is holy. What is most real may be those very things which cannot be expressed at all but only known.

The experience of immeasurable realities is far more important than we might imagine. The things we cannot measure may be the things that ultimately sustain our lives. Much recent medical research suggests that isolation makes us vulnerable to illness and that relationship furthers survival. Medical science has demonstrated that our simple caring for each other sustains us and enables us to better survive even such physical challenges as metastatic breast cancer. Community heals. Yet when it comes to healing relationship, who's to say that communion isn't as important as community.

A diagnosis of life-threatening illness casts us headlong into the subjective world. People who have sought healing everywhere else are often afraid to look within, afraid to find, at depth, someone insignificant or even unworthy. Yet this is rarely the case. The soul is our birthright. At depth, everyone is beautiful. Often it is the discovery of the "spot of grace" that heralds the beginning of our deepest healing.

WHAT IF GOD BLINKS?

When I was small, God was still discussed in the public schools. I remember one assembly in which our principal, a fundamentalist, delivered a fire-and-brimstone kind of sermon to the entire grammar school. She read a passage from the Bible to us and told us it was important that we kneel and pray three times a day because we needed to remind God that we were there. Thinking back, she may not have said this in so many words, but this is what I took away. You prayed because you had to make Him look at you. If God turned His face from you, she told the hushed assembly of children, you would wither up and die, like an autumn leaf. And this part I am sure of, she actually held up a large dried and withered leaf. Even as a five-year-old it seemed to me that God had a lot of other things on His mind besides me. And in between the times that I was praying, He might blink and then what would become of me? I remember the fear, the enormous terror. *What if God blinks?* I became so obsessed with this question, so fearful, I was unable to sleep.

My parents were young socialists who considered religion to be "the opiate of the masses," and my grandfather, who was a rabbi, was my only connection to a reality larger than social well-being and the class struggle. When I was this small, I actually thought of God as a friend of his, like the men who came over to smoke cigars and play gin rummy in our kitchen with my father.

As these fears were not something I could discuss with my parents, I had to wait until my grandfather visited. It was probably only a few days, but I remember the waiting. I don't think you can feel such anguish and aloneness as an adult. You have to be very young.

When I finally got my grandfather to myself I told him what had happened. Shaking, I asked him the fearful question: "What if God blinks?" and at last my terror overwhelmed me and I leaned against his shoulder and began to cry. My grandfather stroked my hair to comfort me. Despite his gentleness he seemed distressed and even angry.

But in his usual calm way, he answered my question with some questions of his own. "Nashume-le," he said (and by the way, for years I thought that my grandfather's name for me meant "Little Naomi"—it actually means "Little Soul"), "if you woke up in the night in your room, would you know if your mother and father had gone out and left you alone in the house?" Still crying, I nodded yes. "How would you know that?" he asked. "Would you see them and look at them?" I shook my head no.

"Would you hear them?"

"No."

"Could you touch them?"

By then I had stopped crying and I remember puzzling over his questions because it seemed obvious to me that I would simply *know* that I wasn't alone in the house. I told him this and he nodded, pleased. "Good! Good! That's how God knows you're there. He doesn't need to look at you to know that you are there. He just *knows*. In just the same way you know that God is there. You just *know* that He is there and you're not alone in the house."

God's presence in the house is an inner experience that never changes. It's a relationship that's there all the time, even when we're not paying attention to it. Perhaps the Infinite holds us to Itself in the same way the earth does. Like gravity, if it ever stopped we would know it instantly. But it never does.

This inner knowing is a way in which I orient myself, an unfailing point of reference. Its effect on my life is as profound, as deep as gravity's influence on my body. More than anything else, my sense of not being alone in the house has been what has allowed me to accompany people as they meet with pain, illness, and sometimes death.

CONNECTING UP

PERHAPS THE WISDOM lies not in the constant struggle to bring the sacred into daily life but in the recognition that there may be no daily life, that life is committed and whole and, despite appearances, we are always on sacred ground. In the midst of daily living, ritual can become a way of remembering this.

A young patient, newly recovered from surgery, told me this story of preparing food to celebrate the holiday of Passover for her Orthodox Jewish sweetheart and forty of their friends. One of the basic beliefs of Judaism is that the home is sacred ground, a place of religious ceremony and ritual. Many of these rituals involve eating, and range from the simplicity of the washing of hands and the blessing of Sabbath wine and bread to the enormous complexity of the Passover dinner. My patient, who was Jewish by background, was raised by people who had lapsed in their observation of the religion and she had never participated in the preparation of the Passover dinner before. Her young man, however, had celebrated the holiday yearly since infancy and had helped his mother make the same preparations year after year. He knew them by heart and he taught her.

The kosher law prohibits eating milk products with meat products. She was surprised to discover that a traditional Jewish kitchen has four complete sets of dishes, pots, silverware, and cooking tools. One set is used daily for food containing milk, and a complete second set is for foods that contain meat. These dishes are never comingled and her friend had two dishwashers and two sinks in his kitchen. In addition to these two sets of dishes there are two more sets, one for milk and the other for meat, which are used only at the time of Passover. Tradition decrees that at this time the daily dishes and utensils are put away in cabinets that are both separate and sealed shut and the holiday dishes are then brought out to prepare the Passover dinner. It is a formidable undertaking.

All this almost overwhelmed her. "Rachel," she said, "you have never seen so many dishes, pots, knives and forks, and pancake turners. It all seemed really pointless to me, but it was so terribly important to Herbert and I was terrified of making a mistake and ruining things for him. But a really strange thing happened. Sometime in the middle of setting up things, I was standing by myself in the kitchen with my arms filled with the everyday milk dishes, looking around me desperately for some shelf room to be able to seal them away. Every shelf was full. I remember thinking, 'Where am I going to put these daily milk dishes?' and suddenly I was not alone. I had a very real sense of the presence of the many women who had ever asked themselves this very ordinary question, thousands and thousands of them, some young, some old, in tents, in villages, in cities. Women holding dishes made of clay and wood and tin, women dressed in medieval clothing, in skins, in crudely woven fabrics and styles I had never seen. Among them were my own grandmothers who had lived and died in Warsaw before I was born.

"In that same instant I also knew that if the human race continued there would be women dressed in fabrics I could not even imagine, holding dishes made of materials not yet invented, who would be standing in their kitchens facing this same problem. Women who had not yet been born. They were there too. In the blink of an eye, alone in Herbert's kitchen, I was in the company of women across more than five thousand years. And too, at that very moment all over the world there were women asking themselves this very question in every human language, 'Where do I put these daily milk dishes?' And I was among them, too.

"Well, Rachel, I almost dropped the dishes, I was so surprised. And it is hard to put it into words, but this was not just an idea, it was more like a happening. I had this vast perspective. I knew myself to be a thread in a great tapestry woven by women in the name of God since the beginning. You would think this would make you feel small, but it didn't. I was a single thread, but I *belonged,* something I had never experienced before. For a few seconds I had a glimpse of something larger, not only of who I am but Whose I am. It only lasted for a second, but I can remember it very clearly. I feel changed by it."

Judaism considers food a visible manifestation of the covenant between man and God. There is a special way to prepare the food as well as special dishes on which to eat specific sorts of food; special blessings to be said over the food and over the cooking. In the life of a woman who prepares food in this way and maintains the kosher kitchen with all its ritual complexity, God can become almost as tangible as the stove.

PRAYER

A PATIENT OF MINE who is very ill was recently told by his oncologist that there was nothing more that could be done for him. The physician then said, "I think you'd better start praying." For this doctor, prayer has become a kind of last resort, something to offer his patients when he runs out of ways to help them personally, when there are no more effective treatments. God has become his final referral.

But prayer is not a way to get what we want to happen, like the remote control that comes with the television set. I think that prayer may be less about asking for the things we are attached to than it is about relinquishing our attachments in some way. It can take us beyond fear, which is an attachment, and beyond hope, which is another form of attachment. It can help us remember the nature of the world and the nature of life, not on an intellectual level but in a deep and experiential way. When we pray, we don't change the world, we change ourselves. We change our consciousness. We move from an individual, isolated making-things-happen kind of consciousness to a connection on the deepest level with the largest possible reality. And then the question "How did you become well?" becomes more a question about mystery than about efficacy. A very different kind of question.

At its deepest, prayer is a statement about causality. Turning toward prayer is a release from the arrogance and vulnerability of an isolated and individual causality. When we pray, we stop trying to control life and remember that we belong to life. It is an opportunity to experience humility and recognize grace.

Sometimes the most powerful prayers are also the most simple. Once, when I was lying on an operating table waiting for anesthesia, one of my surgeons took my hand and asked if I would join him and his operating team in a prayer. Startled, I nodded. He gathered the team around the operating table for a moment of silence, after which he quietly said, "May we be helped to do here whatever is most right."

This traditional American Indian prayer seems such a simple way of relinquishing ultimate causality. By means of it, in an operating room equipped with the latest technology, we were not alone in the house. The comfort my surgeon offered me was very genuine. I felt my fears about outcome slip away and went under anesthesia holding on to those few words with the deepest sense of peace. Like all genuine prayers, this prayer is a powerful way of embracing life, finding a home in any outcome, and remembering that there may be reasons beyond reason.

Prayer is a movement from mastery to mystery. I used to

pray for my patients. These days I pray for myself, too. Sometimes I pray for compassion, but more often I pray for harmlessness, the great spiritual quality embodied in the Hippocratic oath. As a human being, I know I can never hope to have the depth and breadth of perspective to know whether any of my actions will ultimately harm or heal. Yet it is my hope I may be used to serve a holy purpose without ever knowing. So sometimes, before I see a patient I offer up a little wordless prayer: Understanding the suffering is beyond me. Understanding the healing is, too. But in this moment, I am here. Use me.

GRANDMOTHER EVE

When I was small, my grandfather used to tell me stories. Many of these were about women who had lived long ago, heroic women who learned important things through their mistakes. There was Sarah, whose husband's name was Abraham; Rachel, whose husband's name was Jacob; and Esther, who was a queen. It was only after his death that I found out that these stories were Genesis, told by a scholarly, white-bearded Orthodox rabbi to a devoted granddaughter, the child of two young agnostic socialists.

My grandfather's story of Grandmother Eve and the snake is really a story about the importance of the inner life.

In the beginning of the story Grandmother Eve is a little girl and she lives much as I did then, as a child. God is the Father, and like all fathers, He provides food and shelter and all the things necessary to life. In return, Eve obeys Him in the same way I was expected to obey my own daddy.

Life goes on in the garden, much the same from day to day. Very little is asked of Eve. All the animals and plants live there together with Eve, including a tree of great beauty in the center of the garden called the Tree of God's Wisdom. God has offered Eve some very clear guidelines about this tree. She can eat the fruits of all the other trees, but the fruit of this tree is forbidden. In the beginning she accepts this without question, even though the very purpose of life may be to grow in wisdom. As time goes by, even though the garden does not change, Eve changes. She begins to grow up, to become a teenager. One day, as she is passing the most beautiful tree, a snake coiled in its branches speaks to her. "Eve," he says, "here is one of the apples of this tree. Why not eat it?"

At this point my grandfather would always explain that the snake was not really a snake but a symbol for the human yearning for wisdom, the seductive power of the unknown, and the endless fascination that the mysterious has for human beings. The snake is the first teacher, and he addresses that part of Eve which is no longer a little girl, but is a seeker.

Eve thinks back upon what God the Father said. The fruit of the tree is forbidden. But Eve is an adolescent. Like most people her age, she needs to find out for herself. She feels the magnetism of the apple. Drawn toward it, she reaches out for it, takes a bite of it.

The food we eat becomes a part of every one of our cells and is woven into the very fabric of our being. "This apple is no different from any other food," said my grandfather. When Grandmother Eve eats it, the wisdom of God becomes a part of her inner life, a holy wisdom she carries inside her and not something she speaks to outside of herself. She now carries the voice of God inside every one of her cells like a little compass. As her descendants, so do we.

Eating the apple made possible an enormous change in Grandmother Eve's lifestyle. She no longer needed to live in God's house in the nursery in order to be safe. She was able to leave this protected environment because she carried God with her. She could hear Him if she was willing to listen. When she ate the apple she became an adult, and gained the freedom of an adult to go out into a world of complexity, adventure, responsibility, and change. To have her own life and make her own choices.

Like most children, the literal aspects of the story bothered me. "Why, Grandpa," I asked, "did God tell Grandma Eve that she mustn't eat the apple in the first place if it wasn't true?" One of the finest things about my grandfather was that he did not change his response to a question just because the person asking was very young. He answered me as if I were a fellow kabalist. "Nashume-le," he said, "this is a most difficult question, a question worthy of much thought. The Bible is full of the images of God. God as an authoritarian father, God as a lover, God as angry, God as jealous, God as faithful, God as loving. In one place God is walking on the earth and in another His breath blows over the waters. In yet another He is a pillar of fire. But God is none of these things. These are all images of God in the minds of men. Knowing God may require us to question all of these things."

The God within seemed to require a day-to-day, moment-to-moment sort of inner attention rather than just a simple obedience. I felt sorry for Grandma Eve. It seemed much harder than obedience to me.

The complexity of the real world requires us to struggle to hear the Holy and develop a personal responsibility to live a good life. It demands that we stay awake. Grandfather presented Eve to me as a grown-up rather than a sinner. It was years before I heard the official version of the story.

Perhaps there is something for us now in my grandfather's version of the story. We have expected a great deal of our experts and authorities, our doctors, our politicians, our technicians and our educators, even our rabbis, ministers, and priests. We have offered them obedience for the hope that they would become responsible for providing us with a good life. It is time to find the spot of grace within.

THE RABBI'S RABBI

As a young pediatrician, I had as a patient a twelve-year-old girl with Hodgkin's disease, a cancer of the lymph nodes, who had come from New York City for radiation treatment at the Stanford linear accelerator. Her father, an Orthodox rabbi, was deeply traditional and obeyed all of the many rituals and laws of this ancient religion. For the Orthodox, the holiest day of the year is Yom Kippur, the day of atonement for sins committed. On this day, among other things, money is not handled, the skins of animals and even leather shoes are not worn, and one does not ride in cars or use electricity for any purpose. Shoshana's eighth treatment fell on Yom Kippur. The accelerator was too far for this ill young girl to reach by walking and her father came to see me to discuss this. He explained the importance of the meticulous observance of Yom Kippur. He proposed skipping the treatment.

"No," I said. "The timing of these treatments is critical to Shoshana's recovery." Angrily he said that she was not to go. God's laws superseded any human law. I was horrified. "Are you telling me that God's law is more important than your child's treatment? What sort of a God would ask this?" Offended, he quoted the story of Abraham and Isaac to me. I remained unconvinced. He left the office saying that he would refer the matter to a higher authority, the rabbi in New York City who headed his sect of Orthodox Judaism. My heart sank.

But on the morning of Yom Kippur, Shoshana was sitting in her usual place in the waiting room, on time. With her were her mother *and* her father. "I am surprised to see you here, Rabbi," I said. "What did the rabbi in New York say?" Subdued, he told me that he had written to describe the situation and his Rabbi, the Great Teacher himself, had called him. He had told him to order a taxi to come to his home on the morning of Yom Kippur. When the taxi arrived, Shoshana was to ride to her treatment and he was to accompany her.

When he protested riding in a car on Yom Kippur, his Rabbi had insisted he accompany his daughter. "Why is this?" I asked. In a soft voice he said that his Rabbi, the Great Teacher, had insisted that he accompany his daughter so that she would know that even the most pious and upright man in her life, her father, may ride on the holiest of days for the purpose of preserving life. He said that it was important that Shoshana not feel separated from God by this breaking of the law. Such a feeling might interfere with her healing.

SANCTUARY

My cat Charles, who is eighteen years old, has many hiding places. When he is in one of these a subtle change comes over him. No longer is he vigilant and wary, assessing the environment for its potential threat. In his hiding places, he seems at peace and unafraid.

These places are many and varied. Some are classic feline sanctuaries: under the bed, behind the drapes, or in the closet. Others are unique to the house we share: the nook under the stairs or the place behind the television. But one of them is in plain sight, a spot on the living room rug. When Charles is in this spot, he draws about himself the usual inviolateness of all his other hiding spaces. No matter if the delivery man, the neighbor kids, or even the vet comes. In full view he is calm and relaxed. He is himself. He seems so safe there that, watching him, you would think that he is alone.

In a book about Spain, I remember reading an interesting thing about bullfighting. There is a place in the bullring where the bull feels safe. If he can reach this place, he stops running and can gather his full strength. He is no longer afraid. From the point of view of his opponent, he becomes dangerous. This place in the ring is different for every bull. It is the job of the matador to be aware of this, to know where sanctuary lies for each and every bull, to be sure that the bull does not occupy his place of wholeness.

In bullfighting the safe place is called the *querencia*. For humans the *querencia* is a place in our inner world. Often it is a familiar place that has not been noticed until a time of crisis. Sometimes it is a viewpoint, a position from which to conduct a life, different for each person.

Often it is simply a place of deep inner silence.

One of the meditations I have done with people with cancer begins with the suggestion "Find a safe place." A man newly diagnosed with colon cancer once told me the following:

"I never got into the exercise because I could not find a safe place to begin. I looked everywhere. I imagined myself in my home. I imagined myself trout fishing. I imagined myself behind my desk at my business or at the head of the table in the boardroom. Nothing helped. In the midst of this I realized this sort of searching was familiar; I've been doing it all of my life. I began to feel desperate. In the end, I imagined myself a little boy in my mother's arms.

"This last helped. Slowly I began to feel calmer, to get quieter inside, and when at last I felt safe I suddenly knew that the arms around me were not my mother's but my own. The place of safety is inside me. Not outside where I have been looking all my life. All those hiding places, all those achievements. It's inside me. That's why I never found it before."

In working with people with cancer, I have seen the change which happens when a person finds their *querencia.* In full view of the matador, they are calm and peaceful. Wise. They have gathered their strength around them. The inner silence is more secure than any hiding place.

Perhaps this is why the silence in the giant redwood forest near my home draws me. Many mornings I get up early and dress hurriedly to get to the woods before the tour buses and the cars arriving with people from all over the world, come to marvel at the majesty of nature. At eight in the morning, the great trees stand rooted in a silence so absolute that one's inmost self comes to rest. An aged silence. The grandmother of silences. I find the silence even more remarkable than the trees.

Some mornings I sleep through two alarms and awaken only after the first buses have arrived. I go anyway. There are hundreds of people in the woods before me. People speaking French, German, Spanish; people marveling to each other and calling to their children in Japanese, Swedish, Russian, and some languages I do not know. And children shrieking in the universal language of childhood. But the silence is always there, unchanged. It is as impervious to these passing sounds as the trees themselves.

As I age I am grateful to find that a silence has begun to gather in me, coexisting with my tempers and my fears, unchanged by my joys or my pain. Sanctuary. Connected to the Silence everywhere.

CONSECRATING THE ORDINARY

IT IS SAID THAT the Christian mystic Theresa of Avila found difficulty at first in reconciling the vastness of the life of the spirit with the mundane tasks of her Carmelite convent: the washing of pots, the sweeping of floors, the folding of laundry. At some point of grace, the mundane became for her a sort of prayer, a way she could experience her ever-present connection to the divine pattern which is the source of life. She began then to see the face of God in the folded sheets.

People can most easily recognize mystery when it presents itself in dramatic ways. The person who heals for unknown reasons when all hope is gone, the angelic visitation, the life-altering coincidence. We seem to be able to hear God best when He shouts: even Moses required a burning bush, and Jesus' disciples needed him to feed multitudes with a single fish. Yet mystery is as common as a trip to the grocery store. In *Guide for the Perplexed,* E. F. Schumacher notes that the endless debate about the nature of the world is founded on differences in the sensitivity of the eyes that behold it: "We can see only what we have grown an eye to see." Some of us can only notice miracles. Some of us can only see in times of crisis. Yet we can all learn to see God in the folded sheets.

Soon after I moved to California from New York, I planted a vegetable garden. I had never seen fresh vegetables except in a supermarket, and the first year I found an endless fascination in this tiny garden. I especially loved the lettuce which I had planted tightly in a square whose edges I harvested for dinner every night. One evening, I had gone out to pick the salad as usual and ran a hand lightly over the crisp green square of lettuce leaves, marveling at its vitality, almost as if it were bubbling up out of the ground. Suddenly words from my childhood came back to me, words that I had heard countless times over the dinner tables of aunts and uncles and knew by heart, words that I heard now for the first time:

Blessed art Thou, O Lord, King of the Universe who bringest forth bread from the earth.

Far from being the usual meaningless mumble, these words suddenly were a potent description of something real, a statement about grace and the mystery of life itself. Up until then I had taken this blessing as a theory or a hypothesis, someone's idea of how things worked. I had no idea that these familiar words were simply a description of something true. I had never witnessed them happening in the world before.

I had done ritual the way I had done life. Automatically. Life can become habit, something done without thinking. Living life in this way does not awaken us. Yet any of our daily habits can awaken us. All of life can become ritual. When it does, our experience of life changes radically and the ordinary becomes consecrated. Ritual doesn't make mystery happen. It helps us see and experience something which is already real. It does not create the sacred, it only describes what is there and has always been there, deeply hidden in the obvious.

ONE OF A KIND

In a first-growth redwood forest the great trees meet far above, shutting out much of the sunlight. Many of the plants that grow abundantly only a few miles away do not grow here. On the mountain, leaves go every which way. Here in the semi-darkness, all leaves are spread wide and turned up. Even the small plants spread their leaves, the milkmaids and the modesty and the redwood sorrel, which looks like a big clover. Some of the larger plants have leaves as big as dinner plates which float parallel to the ground. When it grows darker, plants turn their leaves up in order to survive and grow. People too. Many of my patients are people whose leaves have turned up.

After all these years of listening it seems to me that the essential quality of the human soul is uniqueness. Each of us is one of a kind. None of us has existed in the history of the human race before. This same realization came to a CEO who is recovering from prostate cancer, in his morning meditation. Just as a simple thought: "I am me," which was followed by a profound sense of peace and an unfamiliar acceptance of himself as he is. He was so surprised he wrote me about it:

"I am shocked to have discovered this morning that I am the only me there is. I think this is the key to everything—compassion, kindness, trust of life, mystery. A genuine and not inflated sense of importance and self-value. I've spent most of my life comparing myself to other men. Are they ahead of me in *Forbes?* Do they sit on more powerful boards? Are they smarter? Sexier? Do they have more hair? And all the time there is this other way of seeing things. I am not one of the motors my company produces by the hundreds of thousands. I am handmade. Less than perfect but more a work of creation than a product of technology. And I am not alone in this. Everyone is the only 'me' there is."

Some insights are visceral. They can change us as profoundly as experience does. Months later this man finds he looks at others differently, listens to them with a new and effortless respect, wants to know the ways in which they are unique. What he used to perceive as differences to be judged and possibly dismissed he now sees as uniqueness to be appreciated and understood. He has learned a great deal of value from people whom he would barely have noticed before. He makes fewer comparisons. And people talk to him differently as well.

Another patient, a man of a far more pragmatic and concrete turn of mind, gained a similar appreciation in a different way.

He entered the elevator of a major hospital on his way to his daily radiation treatment and saw that another man was already there. As they rode up together, my patient had this strange thought:

"How easy it would have been for us to have missed each other. Had he not found that very parking spot and had to ride about a little more, or if this had been a bad day and I couldn't walk as fast, we would not be standing here together. Or if he had found his spot but had stopped for a paper, or if I had stopped for a paper, our lives would not have connected."

And then he just kept going. "What if I had not gotten into Yale and had not met the teacher that inspired me to become a statistician? I would most likely be doing something else, living somewhere else right now. Or if just one more person had applied for my job, who was better qualified than I am, I would not be here in California either. Or if my mother had never met my father, or my grandmother my grandfather, and so on down the line into the unimaginably distant past. If any of these people had missed each other, had made a slight turn to the left or to the right, which could have happened as easily as I could have bought a paper and missed him this morning, I would never have been born. And the same is true for him, one misstep and he would not have been born either. Yet in spite of the most incredible odds, here we are together."

As a statistician, he was moved, overwhelmed by a glimpse of the dance circumstances that had created the occasion of this encounter with a total stranger. And then he remembered what he had said at this extraordinary moment of meeting: "Excuse me, but would you please press ten?"

This man too has been changed by his experience. He finds himself more open to hidden possibilities. More appreciative of the presence of others in his life, more curious about what possible meaning or teaching may be there in the most ordinary of relationships. "It's as if something shook me by the shoulder and said, 'Wake up! There may be more to life than meets the eye.' "

Neither one of these men would describe his experience as spiritual, yet both seem to me to be experiences of the underlying reality and mystery of the world. Experiences of not being alone in the house.

I am not much of a meditator. No matter. I have come to suspect that life itself may be a spiritual practice. The process of daily living seems able to refine the quality of our humanity over time. There are many people whose awakening to larger realities comes through the experiences of ordinary life, through parenting, through work, through friendship, through illness, or just in some elevator somewhere.

The recognition that the world is sacred is one of the most empowering of the many realizations that may occur to people with life-threatening illness and those close to them, their friends, family or even their health professionals. It is one of the ways that such people heal the community around them. And should they die, it is often the legacy they leave behind.

IX.

Mystery and Awe

IN THE CORNER of the basement of the brownstone where my Uncle Frank lived and had his medical offices, there was a battered wardrobe closet made of heavy cardboard. On Saturday mornings when I was quite small, I often played down there by myself, waiting for my father, who worked as my uncle's X-ray technician. One day, more out of boredom than curiosity, I struggled to open the wardrobe door. The hinges had rusted. Inside, hanging from a hook, was a human skeleton.

I was pleased. After examining it for a long time and admiring the beautiful shapes and ivory softness of its bones and the brass pins which cleverly held them together, I discovered that by standing on a chair I could lift it off the hook and bring it out. It was not very heavy. For a long time it became my playmate, my guest at endless tea parties, the confidant of my secrets. Thinking back, I realize how strange a picture this must have made, but it did not seem odd at the time. Or frightening.

At about this same time, I suffered from a repetitive series of night terrors centered on the dumbwaiter, a common feature of hallways in the apartment houses of the forties. The dumbwaiter was designed for lifting groceries five or six stories from the lobby of the building or lowering garbage to the incinerator in the basement. It was a box that moved up and down a vertical shaft and was operated manually by a rope-and-pulley system. Most of the time when one opened the door, the dumbwaiter box was at the floor of whatever neighbor above or below had most recently used it. My mother would reach into the blackness of the shaft and pull on the ropes until the wooden box appeared.

The black emptiness of the shaft terrified me and for a long time I dreamed of it almost nightly. I was certain that the blackness was alive and that some night it would escape its hiding place and get me. I could not sleep unless a light was on. The night terrors went on until an elevator was installed in the building and the dumbwaiter shaft was sealed up. These fears were a prominent part of the fabric of my life back then. I would tell the skeleton about them during our tea parties. The known was far more comfortable than the unknown, even then.

As a physician, I was trained to deal with uncertainty as aggressively as I dealt with disease itself. The unknown was the enemy. Within this worldview, having a question feels like an emergency; it means that something is out of control and needs to be made known as rapidly, efficiently, and cost-effectively as possible. But death has taken me to the edge of certainty, to the place of questions.

After years of trading mystery for mastery, it was hard and even frightening to stop offering myself reasonable explanations for some of the things that I observed and that others told me, and simply take them as they are. "I don't know" had long been a statement of shame, of personal and professional failing. In all of my training I do not recall hearing it said aloud even once.

But as I listened to more and more people with life-threatening illness tell their stories, not knowing simply became a matter of integrity. Things happened. And the explanations I offered myself became increasingly hollow, like a child whistling in the dark. The truth was that very often I didn't know and couldn't explain, and finally, weighed down by the many, many instances of the mysterious which are such an integral part of illness and healing, I surrendered. It was a moment of awakening.

For the first time, I became curious about the things I had been unwilling to see before, more sensitive to inconsistencies I had glibly explained or successfully ignored, more willing to ask people questions and draw them out about stories I would have otherwise dismissed. What I have found in the end was that the life I had defended as a doctor as precious was also Holy.

I no longer feel that life is ordinary. Everyday life is filled with mystery. The things we know are only a small part of the things we cannot know but can only glimpse. Yet even the smallest of glimpses can sustain us.

Mystery seems to have the power to comfort, to offer hope, and to lend meaning in times of loss and pain. In surprising ways it is the mysterious that strengthens us at such times. I used to try to offer people certainty in times which were not at all certain and could not be made certain. I now just offer my companionship and share my sense of mystery, of the possible, of wonder. After twenty years of working with people with cancer, I find it possible to neither doubt nor accept the unprovable but simply to remain open and wait.

I accept that I may never know where truth lies in such matters. The most important questions don't seem to have ready answers. But the questions themselves have a healing power when they are shared. An answer is an invitation to stop thinking about something, to stop wondering. Life has no such stopping places, life is a process whose every event is connected to the moment that just went by. An unanswered question is a fine traveling companion. It sharpens your eye for the road.

As a freshman in medical school I had been randomly selected as class photographer and given a camera to take pictures for the yearbook. I took pictures for four years. At first I felt burdened by the responsibility, the need to carry the heavy camera with me to class, to remember to look at things. But in time, the camera caused me to see my ordinary surroundings far more clearly, to become aware of beauty around me in some very unlikely places. It had given me new eyes. A good question is like that Zeiss.

In some fairy tales there is a magic word which has the power to undo the spell that has imprisoned someone and free them. When I was small, I would wait anxiously until the prince or the princess stumbled on the formula and said the healing words that would release them into life. Usually the words were some sort of nonsense like "Shazam." My magic words have turned out to be "I don't know."

FREEDOM

I WAS JUST beginning my private practice as a counselor to people with cancer when a patient of mine died. He was young, a forty-year-old engineer with cancer of the pancreas. He was referred to me by his oncologist, who said, "Look, I've run out of treatment. I'm willing to talk to him, but I really have nothing more to offer him." Knowing this doctor to be a kind man, I realized that he simply did not know that he had anything other than his expertise that might be of value to his patient. So I said that I would be willing to talk to this man for whom there was no further treatment.

Shortly afterwards, we started our sessions. Richard was a reserved man, very tall and gaunt. He was always carefully and impeccably dressed. The clothing he wore was made to fit the much larger man he once was. I was struck, as I often am when people are this sick, by the iron will that kept him going. He had refused my offer to visit him at his home, insisting that he would come to my office. Later his family told me that it took him more than two hours to dress himself. Refusing their help, he would put on one shoe, then rest, then struggle with the other.

We did four or five sessions together in all. We talked about many things: about his symptoms and his bitterness over what had befallen him, about his feelings of isolation from the people around him, about opening communications with his family. Once or twice, his family came and we all talked and it helped.

One day as he came in he asked me if I would write him a prescription. "Are you in pain?" I asked, my heart sinking. Had his complex regime of pain control lost its effectiveness? It was all we had. He shook his head. "No," he said. "I'm just anxious all the time. I haven't been able to sleep for two nights. I just lie there. Can you give me something?"

I said that I could and asked him if he had any idea what was causing this. "You've been through so much," I told him. "Why now?"

He had no idea.

Had he been having dreams? "Just the one," he told me. In it a ravenous beast was pursuing him. He had not been able to see it but had simply known that it was there. He had awakened, sweating, but he could not remember anything more. I waited for him to continue but he had not made a connection between the dream and what he was feeling.

"Perhaps we should revisit that dream," I suggested. "It may help us to understand." He nodded his agreement. I suggested then that he close his eyes, take a few deep breaths, and let me know when he felt ready to begin. When he signaled his readiness, I asked him to imagine himself back in his dream. This proved surprisingly easy for him. In his imagination, he started to run. In the next ten or fifteen minutes I did everything I knew to help bring him into another relationship with the beast that was pursuing him, to free him of being its prey. Nothing worked. "Become invisible," I suggested.

"It can see me."

"Hide behind something."

"It knows where I am."

"Talk to it."

"It won't answer me." As it gained on him, his anxiety grew.

As it became clear that he would not be able to evade the beast, I began to ask him questions about it. He still could not see it and continued to run, but gradually his answers helped him to know a great deal more about it. He told me that it was irresistible and merciless. There was no negotiating with it. It was "inevitable." But it was not evil. He was very clear about that. In fact, he said it seemed to him to be natural. After some time I said to him, "You know, Richard, you have tried everything. Maybe the only thing left for you to do is to allow it to eat you."

I had expected him to object, to talk about the things he was attached to, the people he would leave behind, but he immediately moved in this direction and imagined himself overtaken. For a while things became intense; Richard sat with his eyes closed, weeping, sweating, and shaking so forcefully I could hear his chair rocking. He seemed far too frail for this and I began to doubt the wisdom of this thing. But slowly the shaking stopped, and he grew calm. Gradually the room became deeply still and in the stillness I had the impression of sunlight, but I knew it was almost five o'clock. Suddenly I remembered the little boy with leukemia who had seemed to know he was going home. I could see him clearly, sitting cross-legged on his bed pillow and smiling at me.

Richard seemed completely relaxed and at peace. So was I. We sat there together for a while and then he said softly, "There is light, there is only Light. I am Light." We sat for a while longer, and then he opened his eyes and said, "Hey, I don't feel anxious at all. That was great, Doctor." The session was over and he left. I had forgotten to give him a prescription for tranquilizers and he had not reminded me.

I was still new to this sort of counseling and for the next three or four days I kept thinking about the session. Intellectually, I suspected that Richard's anxiety had something to do with what Freud calls the fear of Non-Being. But Richard's dream experience seemed different, similar to some other things I had recently read about near-death experience, things that were not yet in the medical literature.

Finally, I called Richard at home and told him I had been thinking about him. "How are you doing?" In a conversational and pleasant voice, he told me that he was doing much worse. He started to describe his new symptoms, yet he seemed calm about these very major physical changes. I pointed this out to him. "Yes, I feel different. That was a helpful session."

"How are you spending your time?"

"Just thinking about things."

"What sort of things?"

He laughed. "Crazy ideas."

"Tell me one."

And he told me that the day before, he had been lying in bed, thinking about getting up, and suddenly out of the corner of his eye he had become aware of some sort of a barrier or a wall just behind him. As he noticed it, he realized that he had always known it was there but he had never seen it before. I encouraged him to say more. "Well, I know I'm here on this side of it. But at the same time, I know I'm on the other side of it too. I don't know what that means. Do you?"

"No," I said.

"Well, I think about it a lot and it makes me feel good. It gives me that same feeling I had in your office. Sort of peaceful and joyful."

"That's a good feeling to have," I told him.

"Yes," he said.

There was a silence and very softly he started to laugh and hung up the phone. Two or three days later, I heard that he had died. I like to think he died a little differently than he might have. I like to think that, but I don't know. I can still hear his laugh.

THE QUESTION

For the last ten years of his life, Tim's father had Alzheimer's disease. Despite the devoted care of Tim's mother, he had slowly deteriorated until he had become a sort of walking vegetable. He was unable to speak and was fed, clothed, and cared for as if he were a very young child. As Tim and his brother grew older, they would stay with their father for brief periods of time while their mother took care of the needs of the household. One Sunday, while she was out doing the shopping, the boys, then fifteen and seventeen, watched football as their father sat nearby in a chair. Suddenly, he slumped forward and fell to the floor. Both sons realized immediately that something was terribly wrong. His color was gray and his breath uneven and rasping. Frightened, Tim's older brother told him to call 911. Before he could respond, a voice he had not heard in ten years, a voice he could barely remember, interrupted. "Don't call 911, son. Tell your mother that I love her. Tell her that I am all right." And Tim's father died.

Tim, a cardiologist, looked around the room at the group of doctors mesmerized by this story. "Because he died unexpectedly at home, the law required that we have an autopsy," he told us quietly. "My father's brain was almost entirely destroyed by this disease. For many years, I have asked myself, 'Who spoke?' I have never found even the slightest help from any medical textbook. I am no closer to knowing this now than I was then, but carrying this question with me reminds me of something important, something I do not want to forget. Much of life can never be explained but only witnessed."

WHAT IS THE SOUND OF ONE HAND CLAPPING?

"FOR EVERYTHING that happens in this world, children, there are two reasons: the good reason and the real reason." Mrs. Mullins, my fourth-grade teacher, was a salty lady and many of her remarks were as cynical as this one. Often her class was too young to understand her meaning, and fearful of missing something important, I had written some of them down. Two decades later I found this one in a notebook in my own childish scrawl. I was a young physician, pretty cynical myself by then, and I chuckled at my old teacher's assessment of the deviousness of the world and assumed that one of the two reasons was false. Now, almost five decades later, I suspect actually both are true.

At the heart of every story is Mystery. The reasons we attribute to events may be far different from their true cause. Often our first interpretation of events is quite different from

our last reading of them. Mystery is a process, and so is our understanding of it.

The ability to seek and find meaning in life is based more than anything on the capacity to hold paradox and maintain an unblushing cognitive dissonance. The objective world and the subjective world lie one atop the other. Spiritual causality and immediate causality are often different yet occupy the same space, and so truth may be less a matter of either/or than both/and. So perhaps Mrs. Mullins was wiser than she knew. For everything that happens in this world there *are* two reasons: the good reason and the Real reason.

Consider the Zen practice of the koan, the question or problem posed by Zen masters to each other or by masters to students. The koan is a dilemma, a mystery which the rational mind cannot solve. By frustrating and thwarting our usual strategies of obtaining answers, knowing and understanding, it causes us to begin anew. The key to the resolution of a koan is a shift in the being of the student which allows for a new understanding of the question itself.

In presenting a koan, the teacher engages the student with mystery in a highly personal way. The student becomes intimate with the question, and sometimes struggles with it for a very long time. At first Zen students respond to the mystery much as we all do: with frustration, with outraged pride, with a sense of unfairness and victimhood, with self-pity, even with anger toward the teacher. None of this works. Having exhausted all these ways, we can begin to find the capacity for other ways and these new ways begin to change us. By putting the habitual mind into a place of stuckness, a sort of fruitful darkness, we may inad-

vertently step back into that fertile and pregnant place of not-knowing called in Zen "beginner's mind."

Mystery can present in very ordinary ways. I didn't always know this. In the early days of my counseling practice I had a remarkable woman as a client. A gifted artist and sculptor, she had gradually become addicted to alcohol. Many years ago, when she hit bottom, her four children were taken from her and given to her mother to raise. Eventually she went into treatment and with great personal strength began a long-lasting recovery and built a productive life of service.

Now in her early fifties, she carried a great deal of responsibility at work and had a lovely apartment of her own.

After several months of sessions, she seemed on the verge of living more openheartedly and I felt this could represent a profound healing for her. At the time, friends of mine were involved in a spiritual practice to open the heart. I called them and asked them to teach me the "heart meditation" which had been so helpful to them. During one of her next visits, I taught this meditation to her and went over it with her very carefully. It took the entire session, but I felt it had been worth it. I reminded her of the importance of doing the meditation every day. She said that she would.

A week later things seemed unchanged. I asked if she was doing the heart meditation. Sheepishly she said that she had only done it once. So we spent the remainder of the session going over it again. The following week she returned anxious and distressed. I asked once again about the meditation. No, she had not done it at all. In annoyance she said that she was not really very interested in doing it, that there was another issue that was

troubling her. She would rather talk about that than the heart meditation now.

In a shaky voice she told me that in the past few weeks a rat had invaded her apartment. She felt it was unclean, even vicious, and it upset her that such a thing could enter the beautiful space that she had so painstakingly created for herself. Despite the obvious importance of this to her and its possible symbolic value, I was frustrated. At the time, I had a very limited sense of the elegance of the spiritual and the many ways it may show itself. Talking about the heart was far more important to me and I thought this rat was in my way. With a sigh I said, "Tell me more."

She became increasingly upset as she talked. She had felt unable to personally set a trap, so she had asked her son if he would come and do this for her. He had but it hadn't helped. The rat still came nightly. The people at work had also tried to be helpful. One of the women had even brought some of the bait she had used when mice invaded her garage. That hadn't worked either. Finally, she had asked the super of the building to inspect her apartment. He had spent a morning covering over all the possible entry points he could find, but the rat was still there. By this time she was almost in tears. In my impatience, I hardly noticed.

"What have *you* done about it?" I asked her. It turned out that other than putting away the edibles she had not really done very much. Finally becoming attentive, I was struck by the number of other people who had become involved. Somewhat unkindly I pointed this out. "I think this is your rat," I told her. "It will probably be there until you personally do something about

it." The minute the words were out I regretted them. They had been harsh and filled with judgment.

For a week I felt badly. I had been unsympathetic and caught up in my own agenda. But she returned for her next appointment, radiant. Encouraged and undaunted, I asked her if she had done the heart meditation. It had completely slipped her mind. But a lot had happened. She told me that when she left she had been so hurt and angry that she thought she would not come back. She had been angry for days. Then she had begun to wonder if there might be something to what I was saying. So she had gone to the hardware store to see if they had a trap that would not hurt the rat. She bought something called, unbelievably, a Hav-a-Hart trap, but couldn't bring herself to use it. Traps were "just not her thing." She had felt completely overwhelmed. "I'm just too *softhearted,*" she told me. Finally it came to her that if it really was her rat, why, she could deal with it in her way. She had gone to the pound and found a kitten that no one wanted and brought it home. She had not seen the rat since.

Her eyes became wet. She had not had a pet since she was four, when her father had brought home a puppy. She had loved it. Her mother had told her she could have it if she took care of it herself. But four is far too young for that sort of thing. She had tried, but the puppy was too much for her. Her mother had a hot temper, especially when she was drinking. One day the puppy would not stop barking and whining and she could not understand what it wanted and calm it. Enraged, her mother had taken it into the bathroom and drowned it.

I was stunned. Softly she told me that she had always believed this was her fault, that she had not loved the puppy well

enough. But the kitten was doing well, it was growing, and every day when she came home from work, it came to meet her and rub up against her legs and purr. Finally her tears overflowed. "It really is growing," she said. "Perhaps my love is enough now."

There are many ways to look at this story but it is certainly not a story about rats. The elegance with which life offers a woman who has never trusted her own love an opportunity to experience its power is breathtaking. I like to think of this also as a story about ultimate causality. My sense of timing was true . . . but I went astray in not looking at the events of her life for the ways in which her healing was already in process, in thinking that it was I who needed to open my client's heart. We may not always recognize the ways that healing starts in our lives. The beginning of a greater wholeness may look as different as an opportunity to meet new men, a rat in an immaculate apartment, an odd idea that just won't go away, or an experience that strains our sense of the ordinary to its limits. Collaboration with this process may require a respect for the mystery which is at the heart of all growth.

The resolution of a koan requires a certain trust of mystery, a faith that there is an answer which will come in time. Understanding often requires a retreat into inner stillness, a movement away from frustration toward an expectant listening, an openness to understanding paired with a willingness to go without understanding until you have become ready to receive it. When the answer and the seeker have grown toward one another the answer seems to emerge by itself. The resolution of a koan is usually obvious; it has been staring us in the face all along, but

we have never seen it before. Once glimpsed, it is difficult to believe that we ever saw things another way, and indeed we will never see things in the old way again. Our eyes have been changed by the way in which we have met with the unknown.

Like good science, the resolution of a koan requires a trust in the larger pattern which underlies the happening that the mind does not understand, and the understanding which is gained is often accompanied by a deep appreciation of the elegance of that pattern, the intelligence of the nature of things. A sense of wonder. An appreciation of the very mystery which has frustrated us. A sense of belonging to it.

Many of the problems Life poses us are seemingly without solutions, much like the koans the Zen teacher presents to the student. Yet meaning and wisdom emerge from one of Life's stories much in the way that the resolution of a koan emerges. Awaiting this meaning is almost like awaiting a birth. After we live a story or hear a story we become pregnant with its meaning. Sometimes the pregnancy may take weeks or even years. Often over time, pregnant with one story, we may give birth to many meanings, each one deeper than the one before. Most of the best stories I have ever lived or been told are like this.

Certainly suffering and illness are koans. Life may itself be a koan. Those people who are able to meet with life the way a Zen student meets with a koan will be moved along a spiritual trajectory by events which reduce others to bitterness and defeat. Not only their physical body but the quality of their soul may be changed in the encounter.

IN DARKNESS

LIGHT IN VARIOUS forms is commonly regarded as symbolic of the energies of healing. Many self-help books use the sun in healing meditations and imageries. Those of my patients who have read these books have come to expect light to symbolize the source of their healing. But things are not always as we have come to expect and the mysterious may surprise us as it did these two men.

The first, a salesman, was referred by his physician because his denial of his disease made it difficult for him to take care of himself. Over and over again he would do foolhardy things like lifting heavy boxes soon after abdominal surgery and forgetting his medications when he traveled. Essential treatment had been delayed or even sabotaged several times and he had suffered a great deal of unnecessary illness because of this. Just prior to his visit, he had developed a drug toxicity and all but lost the strength

in his right arm. During the three days it had taken him to notice this he continued to take the medication. He finally called his physician only when his wife pointed out to him that he was dropping things. His doctor had taken him off the offending medication. Frightened by the possibility of permanent damage to the nerve in his arm, he had agreed to seek counseling.

In our initial conversation, he described his cancer as "this black hole in the middle of my life that keeps pulling me in." When an image appears like this in the course of ordinary conversation, it is rarely random and may tell as much about a person's unconscious world, their deepest attitudes and beliefs, as the contents of their dreams. Without our knowing it, the dream-maker in us may whisper our secrets directly to others. Steve's choice of words suggested that he was using all of his strength to resist a pull, not to surrender to the force of the disease in his life. Perhaps for him, paying attention to his symptoms and taking prescribed medications came under the heading of surrender.

I called his attention to the picture in his words and suggested that it might be saying something important about himself and his life. Perhaps so much of his energy was being used up in resistance that it did not leave him a lot left over to live with. He nodded. I asked him what was in the hole. "Just darkness," he said simply. I invited him to explore this with me in his imagination, to allow himself to be pulled into the hole just to see what it was like.

He hesitated only for a moment. Then he closed his eyes and began to enter into his own image. He imagined himself pulled into the hole, into the darkness. The following comments are from my session notes. Each one is separated by several minutes of silence.

There is darkness. *Big* darkness. I am floating.
The darkness is very soft . . . gentle . . . It supports me.
I have no needs here. . . . (Sighs)
I am tired.
I am at rest . . . totally at rest. Every cell is resting,
Every cell is open. I am filling up . . . filling up with life.
I could not fill up because I could not open up . . . let go.
I can open up in the darkness.
Life is everywhere.
Whatever happens, it will be okay. . . .

The second man, caught up in rage at his cancer and its treatment, responded to the question "What do you think may be needed for your healing?" with a terse "Nothing!" Taking his statement at face value, I asked him to describe "nothing" to me. "Unending darkness," he said. Commenting on the power of that image, I encouraged him to close his eyes and allow himself to experience it.

As his face became more and more relaxed, I asked him how he was feeling. Again, these comments from my session notes are each separated by several minutes of silence.

The darkness is all around me. . . .
I'm not falling. It holds me. I am held in darkness.
Wrapped in darkness.
The darkness is . . . soft . . . almost tender. (Sighs)
It's safe here.
I needed to feel safe. I haven't relaxed since I got the diagnosis. (Sighs again) I can rest. I am so tired.
No pain here. No hunger. No need.

I encouraged him to let himself relax fully. Watching him, it was apparent that he had slipped into a light trance or doze. I covered him with a soft wool blanket that I keep in my office. After a while, he commented that he could hear a sound "like a great heartbeat." It was deeply comforting.

I encouraged him to lean up against it. To rest. Soon he began to weep softly, saying, "Mama, Mama."

Another patient with cancer, a woman, told me of a dream. She turns a corner on a familiar street and is suddenly confronted by a black-cloaked figure:

> I call out for help but there is no one. I am utterly alone with this dark figure. As I turn to flee, the cloak is thrown over me. I struggle but there is no one in the cloak, only darkness. It is black, totally black, but somehow I can see . . . not with my eyes . . . the blackness goes on forever. It is very quiet. Completely silent. Velvety. Soft. I am not falling. I am floating in endless darkness. Floating . . .
>
> I am free. There is no gravity. My body does not hurt anymore. (Long pause) The darkness is like love. It's very, very good here. It takes me in exactly as I am. There's no judgment. I am not wrong. I . . . just am.

These patients and the many others who have had such experiences were taken by surprise by the power of their spontaneous imagery and its form. We often think of health and sickness as an expression of the goodness/evil polarity. Most languages reflect this identification. We say "I feel bad" when we

feel sick and "I feel good" when we recover. Darkness and light are a further extension of this polarity: healing, as a function of the good, is associated with light, and sickness, as a function of evil, is associated with darkness.

Darkness has suffered bad press for millennia. Yet is it really so surprising that spontaneous healing imagery may present itself in this way? According to the traditions of alchemy, darkness was the necessary condition for purification and transformation. Alchemists put impure dross metals into a sealed flask, creating the perfect darkness required for the transformation into pure gold.

As light represents the archetype of masculine energy, darkness suggests the power of the feminine, and it makes an intuitive sense that the *experience* of healing may be associated with darkness. Darkness is a condition of the beginning. The body first comes into being in darkness. It is nurtured, as a seed, in darkness. Some people may find their healing in remembering the beginning.

SEEING AROUND THE CORNER

My given name is Rachel. I was named after my mother's mother. For the first fifty years of my life, I was called by another name, Naomi, which is my middle name. When I was in my middle forties, my mother, who was at that time almost eighty-five, elected to have coronary bypass surgery. The surgery was extremely difficult and only partly successful. For days my mother lay with two dozen others in the coronary intensive-care unit of one of our major hospitals. For the first week she was unconscious, peering over the edge of life, breathed by a ventilator. I was awed at the brutality of this surgery and the capacity of the body, even in great age, to endure such a major intervention.

When she finally regained consciousness she was profoundly disoriented and often did not know who I, her only child, was.

The nurses were reassuring. We see this sort of thing often, they told me. They called it Intensive Care Psychosis and explained that in this environment of beeping machines and constant artificial light, elderly people with no familiar cues often go adrift. Nonetheless I was concerned. Not only did Mom not know me but she was hallucinating, seeing things crawling on her bed and feeling water run down her back.

Although she did not seem to know my name, she spoke to me often and at length, mostly of the past, about her own mother who died before I was born and who was regarded as a saint by all who knew her. She spoke of the many acts of kindness which her mother had done without even realizing she was being kind. *"Che-sed,"* said my mother, using a Hebrew word which roughly translates as "loving kindness." The shelter offered to those who had none, the encouragement and financial support which helped others, often strangers, to win their dreams. She spoke of her mother's humility and great learning and of the poverty and difficulty of life in Russia which she remembered as a child. She recalled the abuses and hatreds the family experienced to which many others had responded with anger and her mother only with compassion.

Days went by and my mother slowly improved physically although her mental state continued to be uncertain. The nurses began correcting her when she mistook them for people from her past, insisting that the birds she saw flying and singing in the room were not there. They encouraged me to correct her as well, telling me this was the only way she might return to what was real.

I remember one visit shortly before she left the intensive

care unit. I greeted her asking if she knew who I was. "Yes," she said with warmth. "You are my beloved child." Comforted, I turned to sit on the only chair in her room but she stopped me. "Don't sit there." Doubtfully I looked at the chair again. "But why not?"

"Rachel is sitting there," she said. I turned back to my mother. It was obvious that she saw quite clearly something I could not see.

Despite the frown of the special nurse who was adjusting my mother's IV, I went into the hall, brought back another chair, and sat down on it. My mother looked at me and the empty chair next to me with great tenderness. Calling me by my given name for the first time, she introduced me to her visitor: "Rachel," she said. "This is Rachel."

My mother began to tell her mother Rachel about my childhood and her pride in the person I had become. Her experience of Rachel's presence was so convincing that I found myself wondering why I could not see her. It was more than a little unnerving. And very moving. Periodically she would appear to listen and then she would tell me of my grandmother's reactions to what she had told her. They spoke of people I had never met in the familiar way of gossip: my great-grandfather David and his brothers, my great-granduncles, who were handsome men and great horsemen. "Devils," said my mother, laughing and nodding her head to the empty chair. She explained to her mother why she had given me her name, her hope for my kindness of heart, and apologized for my father who had insisted on calling me by my middle name, which had come from his side of our family.

Exhausted by all this conversation, my mother lay back on her pillows and closed her eyes briefly. When she opened them again, she smiled at me and the empty chair. "I'm so glad you are both here now," she said. "One of you will take me home." Then she closed her eyes again and drifted off to sleep. It was my grandmother who took her home.

This experience, disturbing as it was for me at the time, seemed deeply comforting to my mother and became something I revisited again and again after she died. I had survived many years of chronic illness and physical limitation. I had been one of the few women in my class at medical school in the fifties, one of the few women on the faculty at the Stanford medical school in the sixties. I was expert at dealing with limitations and challenges of various sorts. I had not succeeded through *loving kindness.* Over a period of time I came to realize that despite my successes I had perhaps lost something of importance. When I turned fifty, I began asking people to call me Rachel, my real name.

REMEMBERING THE SACRED

IN RESPONSE TO an invitation to remember a moment in the practice of medicine that might be considered a sacred experience, a seasoned neonatologist, the director of the neonatal unit at a large southern hospital, offered a group of colleagues this account. After weeks of struggle, her patient, a tiny premature baby, was dying despite everything that a state-of-the-art intensive care nursery could offer. It would not be long and it was time for the parents to say good-bye. With a heavy heart she called the baby's father and invited him to meet her at the hospital. The child's mother, distraught after weeks of uncertainty, now required medication. She had stopped visiting a few weeks ago. He would come alone, he said.

As she put down the phone she became aware of the beeping of the monitors and other machines and the bustle of the in-

tensive care nursery and felt the need for some quiet to organize her thoughts while she waited for him to arrive. She went down the hall to the chapel, the only quiet place nearby, to be alone for a few minutes and find words to tell the young father that his little son was not going to make it.

Fifteen minutes later, as she was walking toward the visitors' waiting room, she found herself thinking that perhaps she should give the baby a trial with a certain drug. The thought surprised her, as this drug was not customarily used for the baby's problem, and she shook her head in annoyance. But the strange thought would not easily go away. She reviewed the baby's course with the father, assuring him that everything possible had been done and suggesting they go to the intensive care nursery together to say good-bye. As she looked at the sadness in his face, she found herself thinking, "After all, what does it matter?" and suggested that perhaps there was one more thing she could try, a drug not usually given for this condition, but which she was thinking of using now. She would like to have his permission to use it. He gave this readily and they went to the nursery together.

The baby appeared moribund. Embarrassed to make so unusual a request of the nurses, she prepared the injection and administered it herself. Together she and the father waited, standing on either side of the Isolette, watching the blue and gasping baby. There was no change. Wanting to give him a chance to be alone with his child for the last time, she left to do some paperwork. A few hours later, she looked into the unit and was surprised to see him still there. She approached the Isolette and found that the infant's tiny chest had slowed and his breath-

ing was normal. Scarcely able to believe her eyes, she raised her head and found the father looking at her. Their eyes held for a long, wordless moment. This was the moment she had chosen to tell us about as a "sacred" moment. Recently these parents brought their child back to visit her. He is twelve years old.

The circle of physicians sat thinking about this for a while. Then the neonatologist began to describe the way in which she had dealt with this strange happening at the time. She has a very orderly and pragmatic mind, she told us, and it had disturbed her. She had tried to find an explanation for it so she could dismiss it. Gradually she became convinced that somewhere she had read or heard a preliminary report of research which mentioned the use of this drug for the baby's condition and this was why she had thought of it. She could not remember the journal or the meeting where she had gotten this information, but she became more and more certain that it was so. This allowed her to forget the whole thing.

About two years later, she read of a study of premature infants with severe respiratory distress who had been given this very drug and had recovered. The mystery was solved! Delighted, she called the researchers to ask where they had published their preliminary reports or presented their work in progress. She was stunned to discover that this article was the first time that the study had been written up or presented anywhere. It had just been too odd to talk about until the results were final. She told them then that she had an additional case.

In musing aloud about her personal reactions, she told us that she had clung to an explanation that would have allowed her to keep her familiar and comfortable sense of the way in which

the world works. She had rejected the gift of awe once, so it had to be given to her again.

A second physician, a specialist in palliative care, talked about an experience he had while caring for a hospitalized young man who was dying of AIDS. Both the patient and his family were bitter, rejecting, and hostile despite his efforts to reach out to them. Finally giving up on it, he had simply delivered the best technical care he knew.

At three o'clock one morning he was called by the nurses, who informed him that his patient had died and asked him to come in to pronounce him dead and sign the death certificate. Remembering that he needed to be at rounds very early the next morning, he hastily threw clothes over his pajamas, and began driving to the hospital. As he drove down the darkened streets, he spontaneously looked up and saw the night sky as if for the first time. The darkness seemed a silent and holy emptiness without beginning or end. In this vastness, stars hung as countless pure points of radiance. He had never seen the night in this way and was filled with awe and a profound feeling of peace and gratitude. His intellect attempted to dismiss this as fanciful, pointing out the need to hurry and take care of business so as to be able to get up early the next day. But he stopped his car by the side of the road anyway, got out, and allowed the experience of awe to wash over him. In about fifteen minutes it receded and he drove on to the hospital under a sky that looked much the same as always. The experience had been brief, but powerful and surprisingly important to him although he couldn't say why.

Together the group of physicians considered what this ex-

perience may possibly have meant. Various interpretations were offered, but the one that stopped further conversation was that perhaps the patient, in passing onward, may have found a way to share his present perspective directly with his doctor as an apology and a parting gift. As one of the doctors put it, "Perhaps at the moment of death there is a reclaiming of wholeness . . . and that wholeness may pass very close to us."

MYSTERY

I WAS LATE for what was to be my last visit with my mother. Pushing through rush hour traffic, tired from a long day at the office, I stopped to buy her some flowers. It was seven in the evening and the florist had no purple irises, my mother's favorites, and little of anything else. Sympathizing with my distress, he offered me a bouquet of half-closed iris buds from his icebox, assuring me that they would open in a few hours. I took them and waited, irritated and impatient, as he wrapped them in green tissue. A strange-looking bouquet. Then I hurried on.

Carrying the flowers, I pushed through the heavy doors of the ward. A nurse was waiting there for me. "I'm so sorry," she said. My mother had died a short time before. Stunned, I allowed myself to be led to her room. She lay in her bed, seemingly asleep. Her hands were still warm. The nurse asked if there was anyone I wanted her to call. Numbly I gave her the numbers of

some of my oldest friends and sat down to wait. It was peaceful and very still in the room. One by one my friends came.

Four days later I was three thousand miles away arranging for my mother's burial. It was an unseasonably hot spring and New York City was at its worst, muggy and uncomfortable. The funeral director was a person of sensitivity and kindness. Gently he went over the arrangements, assuring himself and me again of the details of my mother's wishes which we had discussed on the phone. Then he paused. "There was something that came from California with your mother. May I show you?" he asked. Together we walked down the corridor to where my mother lay in her closed pine coffin. Lying on the coffin lid, still in the twist of green tissue paper was the bouquet I had left in my mother's hospital room on her bed. But now the irises were in full bloom. I remember them still with great clarity, each one huge and vibrant, seemingly filled with a purple sort of light. They had been out of water for four days.

It would be easy indeed to dismiss this sort of experience, not to make a simple shift in perspective or find a willingness to suspend disbelief for a moment. Not to consider adding up the column of figures in another way and wonder. The willingness to consider possibility requires a tolerance of uncertainty. I will never know whether or not I was once for a moment in the presence of my Russian grandmother or if my mother used my final gift of flowers to make me a gift of her own, letting me know that there may be more to life than the mind can understand.

THE FINAL LESSON

SOMETIMES the particulars of the way in which someone dies, the time, place, even the circumstances, may cause those left behind to wonder whether the event marks the healing of hidden patterns and personal issues, and answers for that person certain lifelong questions. Death has been referred to as the great teacher. It may be the great healer as well. *Educare,* the root word of "education," means to lead forth the innate wholeness in a person. So, in the deepest sense, that which truly educates us also heals us.

The theory of karma suggests that life itself is in its essential nature both educational and healing, that the innate wholeness underlying the personality of each of us is being evoked, clarified, and strengthened through the challenges and experiences of our lifetime. All life paths may be a movement toward the soul. In which case our death may be the final and most integrating of our life's experiences.

When I met Thomas, he was over seventy, a family-practice physician who had been in solo practice for almost fifty years. Whole families, from grandparents to grandchildren, looked to him for help in their troubles, counted on his counsel, and called him their friend. He looked the part too, gray-haired, kindly, his body as spare and gnarled as an old oak.

At the time that we met, he had end-stage lung cancer. He could no longer get around without the constant flow of oxygen through a nasal catheter, and the previous month he had closed his medical practice. Until the last year he had never missed a day. An astute diagnostician, he had come because he knew he was dying. He proposed that we open a series of conversations about his life. He had done some reflection in recent years but felt that sharing the process at this point might be helpful in readying himself for death.

Thomas felt death to be an unqualified ending to life. Raised a Catholic, he had left the church early and embraced science as a way to bring order to the chaos of life. It had not failed him. Yet life had intrinsic value for him and he wished to examine and understand his own life and what it had meant.

It surprised me that a man this altruistic, compassionate, and reverent toward the life in others, this awed by the beauty of anatomy and physiology, held no religious or spiritual beliefs. Curious, I asked him about the circumstances under which he had decided to leave the church. Open and frank about other details of his long life, he was reticent in the extreme about this. He had left at sixteen over a specific happening. I never found out what it was.

Thomas had been a loner all his life. Never married, he had

led a personal life that was solitary almost to the point of asceticism. Yet he was a connoisseur of beauty in all its forms, a patron of the arts, poetry, theater, music, ballet, and literature. His library held over a thousand books. Thomas's major commitment was to his medicine, his families and their needs, hopes, and dreams. His devotion to them was absolute.

Very early on in our discussions, I asked him how he saw his relationship to his patients. Looking at a small figurine of a shepherd with his flock that another patient had given me, he smiled. "Like that." We spent the next few weeks examining the nature of his work and what it had meant to him. The shepherd was a steward of the life in the flock, he protected them from danger, helped them to find nurture and fulfill themselves. He delivered their young. He found the strays and brought them back to the others.

Thomas told me many stories of his shepherding and the life of his flock. We examined these stories together, sharing our thoughts and perspectives. In the telling and the reflection, he seemed to be unfolding a much deeper sense of what his life had meant to others and what he had stood for. In these discussions, he often used an odd Victorian word: they "sheltered" with him. He was their safety, their support, their friend. He was there for them, constant, vigilant, and trustworthy. We discussed the yang or masculine principle of action and protection and the yin or feminine principle of acceptance and nurture and how these came together in the person of a shepherd. The symbol emerged as a symbol of wholeness.

All the while, he was becoming more and more ill, his breathing more labored. Eventually I raised the issue of his per-

sonal isolation. Who did he shelter with, who was the shepherd's shepherd? "No one," he said, the words holding more pain than he had expressed before. It became clear that he did not believe that there was a place of sheltering for himself. Shepherd though he was professionally, personally he had become separated from the flock, a nonparticipant, a lost person. He seemed unwilling to go much further with this.

Puzzled, I asked him to make up a story about a lost lamb, and haltingly he described a lamb that had been lost for so long that he could not even remember there was a flock. He had learned to survive by himself, to eat what was available, to hide from predators. "Does this lamb know that his shepherd is looking for him?" I asked. "No," he said, "the lamb had done something very bad and the shepherd had forgotten him."

"As a shepherd yourself, would you look for a lost lamb who had done something bad?" He seemed puzzled. I reminded him of the young patient from the projects he had told me about, the one he had taken on as a guardian from the juvenile courts, the girl who eventually went on to college. I asked him why he had gone after her and brought her home. "Why, she was one of mine," he said unhesitatingly. "Yes," I said. There was a small silence. Then he abruptly changed the subject, but I saw he was deeply affected by the thought that the bond between the shepherd and his sheep might lie beyond judgment and was deeper than he had previously thought.

We talked of many other things over the next months and gradually the image of the shepherd retreated to the back of my mind. We spoke of childhood and manhood and lost love, and the richness of seventy years of living became apparent to us both. It had been a good life.

Thomas was hospitalized once and his health continued to worsen. His oncologist had exhausted all treatment for his cancer and began to increase medications to ease his respiratory distress. Gradually he became too ill to come to the office and in the fall I began to see him at his home. Hospice was called and by the beginning of December he had become so short of breath that he could no longer speak. I sat with him and held his hand. Sometimes I would read him poetry or sing to him a little.

Somehow he kept hanging on. The hospice workers were surprised by his endurance. One of his nurses told me that she thought he was waiting for something. I thought perhaps she was right but I had no idea of what it could be. His brother had come from the East Coast to say good-bye and many of his patients had already visited and left cards and other expressions of their love.

On Christmas Eve I received a call from his nurse. Thomas had been in a coma all day and now he was having difficulty with his secretions. Would I come? As soon as I saw Thomas, I realized that he was dying. His breathing, always labored, had become shallow and intermittent. The nurse with him was young and seemed a little uncertain and so I invited her to stay as I talked to him. He did not respond in any way. We changed his sheets and made him more comfortable. Then we sat down together to wait. Gradually the space between his breaths lengthened and after a while his breathing stopped.

The young nurse seemed relieved. She called Thomas's brother, who had asked to be notified and who said that he would fly out the next day. He asked that she call the funeral director Thomas had chosen and she called him, too. She called his oncologist to sign the death certificate. There seemed noth-

ing more to do. I stood for a time at the foot of Thomas's bed, thinking about him and wishing him well. Then I left.

It was dark and had grown quite cold. Holding my keys in my pocket, I huddled into my coat and walked a little faster. I had almost reached my car when church bells throughout the city began ringing. For a moment I stopped, confused. Could they be ringing for Thomas? And then I remembered. It was midnight. The Shepherd had come.

EPILOGUE

Anything that is real has no beginning and no end. The stories in your life and in mine do not stop here. Many kitchen tables await us and over time we may sit again at the kitchen tables of our past. One of my fondest memories is of the Sunday afternoons of my childhood. While the rest of the family would assemble in the living room after lunch, discussing world events and politics, my grandfather and I would meet in the kitchen and talk about God. These meetings were secret, as my parents, proud to be modern, viewed God as slightly more than superstition and laid the solutions to all of life's problems in the lap of science. They would not have been pleased with such talk.

So, as the policies of Roosevelt were hotly debated in the other room and Churchill's speeches were read aloud and admired, my grandfather and I would sit at the kitchen table talking about the holy nature of the world. He would teach me the

special blessings for the many bounties that life offers or read to me from one of the ancient texts he always carried in his pocket. Occasionally he would encourage me to memorize a passage, usually from Psalms or Proverbs or a little book called *Pirkey Avot, Sayings of Our Fathers.* The psalms and proverbs were beautiful and easy to remember, and the blessings too, but the Sayings were difficult for me, as they were complex and subtle, a bit much for a six-year-old. But I could see how much my grandfather loved these words, and supported by his love, I would try to understand them and learn them by heart.

When my attention flagged, my grandfather would encourage me to continue with the tiniest sip of the Manischewitz Sacramental Concord Grape wine which he kept hidden in the back of the refrigerator. It was a blatant bribe. I loved the wine.

I remember struggling with one of the Sayings. It was the Jewish koan:

If I am not for me, then who is for me?
If I am just for me, then who am I?
And if not now, then when?

The words made no sense at all to me, and even my grandfather's patient explanations did not help. Finally I cried out in frustration, "Grandpa, I don't know what it means." "Ah, Nashume-le," he said, "then remember it and wait. Someday if you need to know it, its meaning will come to you." I looked at my beloved grandfather, shocked, seeing for the first time that he was old. Perhaps he would not be with me to share my questions for all of my life. Perhaps someday he would die and I would be alone with them. I burst into tears, overwhelmed.

Manischewitz has bottled wine in the same square bottle for more than seventy years. Many things come close to me whenever I pass a bottle in the supermarket. Perhaps wisdom is simply a matter of waiting, and healing a question of time. And anything good you've ever been given is yours forever.

ACKNOWLEDGMENTS

It actually takes a whole village to write a book.

My gratitude to all those who have shared themselves so generously with me, to the patients who have made me proud to be a human being and the physicians and medical students who have made me proud once again to be a doctor. Thanks to those who have given me their permission to tell their story and to those whose place in the world has become lost to me and whose names, occupations, and diagnoses I have changed so that they alone will know who they are.

My gratitude also to those who made this book a reality: to Esther Newberg, my agent, for the support her unshakable honesty and integrity have offered me and to Dean Ornish, whose friendship has made it all possible. Thanks to Amy Hertz, my editor, for knowing what did not belong and making it stick, and to the wonderful people at Riverhead for taking a chance.

A very special thanks to Barbara McNeill, for the constancy of her faith in this book, her unfailing generosity, and the grace of her unique insights. Thanks also to Tamara Cohen, Judith Skutch-Whitson, Whit Whitson, Lou Carlino, and Jilly Carlino for reading the first draft of the proposal and believing that there was a book in it.

A blessing on John Kabat-Zinn, David Eisenberg, and Charles Terry for knocking down all my intellectual pretensions and encouraging me to write in the same way that I live my life. And another blessing to Laurance and Mary Rockefeller, who believed that I could do it in the first place and whose support gave me the courage to try.

My deepest gratitude to my friend Yola Jurzykowski, for calling from Nepal late one evening and telling me what this book was really about, and to my friends Jenepher Stowell, Marion Weber, Don Flint, Waz Thomas, Marya Marthas, Marilyn Wall, and John Tarrant for listening hour after hour to stories read over the phone, sometimes into the wee hours of the morning.

My special thanks to Janie Siegrist for reading every draft of this book with love and wisdom and praying over them all, and to all the others who waded undismayed through earlier and much bigger forms of the manuscript; Sukie Miller for spending days cutting it up into bits, and Phillip Brooks, Harris Dientsfrey, Josh Dunham-Wood, Don Flint, Waz Thomas, Barbara McNeill, Stephen Mitchell, Jenepher Stowell, and Marion Weber for offering insights and criticisms with such kindness and love. Thanks to Caryle Hirschberg for airlifting me and my editors out of our many jams with Compuserve, and to John Tar-

rant for urging me to abandon Microsoft 6.0 for the Mac and take refuge in WordPerfect 3.1.

My perennial gratitude to Michael Lerner, colleague extraordinaire, and the staff of the Commonweal Cancer Help Program and the Institute for the Study of Health and Illness at Commonweal for their support. A rose to Taylor Brooks, Jnani Chapman, Purusha Doherty, Elizabeth Evans, Don Flint, Irene Gallwey, Monica Kauffer, Lenore Lefer, Shannon McGowan, Elise Miller, David Parker, Nadine Parker, Sharyle Patton, Michael Rafferty, Sara Reingold, Christine Schultz, Jenepher Stowell, Waz Thomas, and Virginia Veach for their kindness all these months to a cranky and distracted person.

My thanks also to those whose commitment and support have created the field which surrounds this work: Rob Lehman and the trustees and staff of the Fetzer Institute, Charles Halpern and the good people of the Nathan Cummings Foundation, Wink Franklin and the board and staff of Institute of Noetic Sciences, and Eileen Rockefeller Growald, the courageous and visionary founder of the Institute for the Advancement of Health.

A heartfelt thanks to Nina Stradtner for creating a place of such lasting peace, order, and calm in my home once a week that it translated effortlessly into a place of calm inside my head.

And lastly, the deepest thanks to those few who knew me before I began to know myself, who believed in me even then and through their own integrity held me to mine: my grandfather, Rabbi Meyer Ziskind, my mother and father, Gladys Sara Remen and Isidore Joseph Remen, and my friends and fellow travelers, Brendan O'Regan and Sara Unobskey Miller.

Without them I would have been a very different story.